Beulah Gary

W9-ACH-235

A GREAT TIME TO BE ALIVE

Other Books

HARRY EMERSON FOSDICK

o

o

A Great Time To Be Alive

Sermons on Christianity in Wartime

by

HARRY EMERSON FOSDICK

PUBLISHERS
HARPER & BROTHERS
NEW YORK AND LONDON

Contents

Contents

Introduction

WITH one exception the sermons in this volume have been preached since the Japanese attack on Pearl Harbor. That exception, "Loyalty, the Basic Condition of Liberty," was preached on the Sunday morning of that fateful day. All these sermons, therefore, have this present war as their background; and they have been selected because, in one way or another, they deal with the problems, personal and public, that the war presents.

Now that the volume is ready for the press, I see that many things needing to be said about Christianity in wartime these particular sermons do not include, but, for what they may be worth, I offer to my friends these twenty-five Sunday morning messages, presented in the Riverside Church, New York, during the momentous months since America's military participation in World War II began.

In necessarily abbreviated form the substance of these sermons has been presented over the Blue Network to the radio audience, and alike for the cordial response of that unseen congregation and for the loyal support of my ministry by the church I serve, I am endlessly grateful.

Mrs. Forrest B. Stannard has been an indispensable help in preparing the manuscript, checking the references, and seeing the volume through the press, and to her I owe my very hearty thanks.

HARRY EMERSON FOSDICK

July 7, 1944.

〜〜〜〜〜〜〜〜〜〜〜〜〜〜〜〜〜〜〜〜〜〜〜〜〜〜〜〜〜〜〜〜〜〜〜〜〜〜〜

Acknowledgments

The author wishes to express his appreciation to the following authors and publishers for permission to quote from their copyrighted works:

Sgt. Hugh Brodie for a poem beginning "Almighty and all present Power."

Mrs. George S. Burgess for "America the Beautiful," by Katharine Lee Bates.

Harper & Brothers for "Dirge Without Music" from *The Buck in the Snow and Other Poems,* by Edna St. Vincent Millay. Copyright, 1928, by Edna St. Vincent Millay.

Harper & Brothers for quotations from *The Bible: A New Translation,* by James Moffatt.

Dorothy Sayers for a poem from *Catholic Tales.*

Charles Scribner's Sons for "The Crystal" from *Poems of Sidney Lanier,* edited by his wife.

A GREAT TIME TO BE ALIVE

A Great Time To Be Alive

THIS certainly is a ghastly time to be alive. Behind the stirring headlines that narrate the clash of armies and the march of victory, an unheralded mass of human misery exists, the like of which our earth has seldom, if ever, seen before. Because of the last war, says Dr. Hambro, late president of the League of Nations, thirty-five million human beings died of starvation and epidemics, but that is only a drop in the bucket compared with this war's disaster. Whether one thinks of what our enemies have done to us—of Warsaw, Lidice, Rotterdam, Coventry—or of what we have done to them—"We drop liquid fire on these cities," says one expert in air warfare, "and literally roast the populations to death" —we are living in a grim and hideous time.

If only we could hope that war would solve the problems it has set out to solve, *that* would redeem, in part at least, our estimation of our era, but war never does that. When this conflict is over and its immeasurable sacrifices have been poured out, Hitler, to be sure, will be gone, but the basic problems that confronted us before, even the fear of totalitarian dictatorship, will confront us still, and endless new problems as well that the war itself has caused. As one of our social research scientists pitilessly puts it: "The war will have solved no basic problems. As a matter of fact, it will have made a good many of them more complicated. . . . To expect otherwise is like expecting that pneumonia will have cured the physical debility that brought it on. You're lucky to be as well off after the siege is over."

Moreover, this is an especially hideous generation for Christians. Ralph Waldo Emerson, when a young minister, attended an important Bible society's convention in a southern state, and by chance the meetings were held in a room whose windows opened on a slave market where Negroes were being auctioned off. So Emerson describes the scene: "One ear therefore heard the glad tidings of great joy, whilst the other was regaled with 'Going, gentlemen, going.' And almost without changing our position we might aid in sending the Scriptures into Africa, or bid for 'four children without the mother' who had been kidnapped therefrom." Such an intolerable contradiction we face now in a generation where one listens with one ear to the faiths, hopes, and ideals of the Christian gospel, and with the other to this war's unbridled violence and brutality.

Recently a woman said, "I adore my children, but lately I have caught myself almost wishing I had never brought them into the world," and a man said, "I am discouraged. All the ideals and values for which I have worked during recent years appear to be losing out." Such moods are natural, for we confront a generation such as faced the writer of the fourth Psalm: "Many there are that say, Who will show us any good?"

Nevertheless, this is also a great time to be alive, and alike the personal and the public issues of it depend on whether we see that.

For one thing, ours is a day when we cannot seek for ease but must seek for adequacy. Life's restful days we love, but other days come too—great days—that require of us not ease but adequacy. Some eras are like a lullaby; some are like a spur. Which of the two is likely in the end to be the greater?

Recently we celebrated the two-hundredth anniversary of Thomas Jefferson's birth. What kind of era did he live in? He thought it appalling. The gains of civilization thrown away, he saw in the early nineteenth century a dismaying renaissance of primitive barbarism: "Those moral principles and conventional usages," he wrote, "which have heretofore been the bond of civilized nations, . . . have given way to force, the law of Barbarians, and the nineteenth century dawns with the Vandalism of the fifth." Yet, looked at now in retrospect, what kind of generation was it in which Thomas Jefferson, George Washington, Alexander Hamilton, John Marshall, and their colleagues, lived? We glory in it! It offered them no ease; it demanded of them adequacy, and, rising to meet it, they made of it a great time.

Surely this thing we are trying to say is true to life both public and personal. Victor Hugo, for example, during his early years enjoyed a happy and resounding success seldom equaled in France—he was the pet of the populace, the pride of the theater, the glory of Paris. Then Napoleon III rose to power, and with superb courage Hugo withstood his growing tyranny. For him ease vanished and tragedy began, until the edict of banishment made him for nearly nineteen years an exile. Of course he hated that deplorable experience, yet out of those years came his greatest work. His biographer calls that fateful period "miraculously inspired," and during it, he says, "books that were far stronger than everything that had gone before, . . . came from his hand," and "he became twice the size of the man he had been." Even Hugo himself exclaimed, "Why was I not exiled before!" What if instead of making such creative response to a tragic time he had settled back, saying, "Who will show us any good?"

Whether or not I am talking to your need, I am talking to my own. I dreaded the coming of this war as one might dread perdition, hating it as the summation of all villainy. War is essentially the denial of everything Christ stood for. For youth it is bad enough, but for an older man too it is a ghastly time to live. Yet that is not the whole story. One who knows history knows that in just such times as these, turbulent and revolutionary, whole generations have been brought to their senses; strong souls called on for adequacy have proved adequate; creative gains have come as from travail, and long afterwards flags have been flown by rejoicing nations because of what was

[3]

done in them. To such a generation it is shameful to make no better response than to cry, "Who will show us any good?"

Our Lord, too, had his hours of serenity and ease when he looked with joy upon the flowers of Galilee and said that "Solomon in all his glory was not arrayed like one of these." But he came at last to another kind of place, where no ease was his but fearful crisis, demanding adequacy, as in Gethsemane he prayed for insight to see, and strength to do, the will of God. That too was a great day.

Not only is this a generation which, if we will, can call out personal adequacy, it is an era also when we cannot remain static, when change is forced upon us, when willy nilly we must make momentous decisions that will affect for good or ill the whole world's future.

Human nature instinctively dislikes change. We love to play safe by staying put. We settle down in a familiar place, clinging even to its faults rather than risking the unknown that alteration brings. There is in humankind a natural timidity that

> ... makes us rather bear those ills we have
> Than fly to others that we know not of.

In church we pray that the world may be saved, but commonly when we leave the church we still try to save the world without changing it. Many Americans today would love to save the world if only they could save it without changing their isolationism, without changing their ideas of absolute national sovereignty, without changing their racial prejudices and their economic ideas to fit the new interdependent world. Then history, tired and impatient of our lethargy and our reluctance to alter anything, hurls us out of our peaceful decades into a maelstrom like this, crying, Now you have got to change! And when that kind of era comes, like it or not, it is a great time to be alive.

The three major forces of our time are fascism, communism,

and democracy, and our main emphasis is on the difference between them. They stand in contrast, their unlikeness stressed and evident. But on one point these three predominant elements in our contemporary world agree: They are at one in demanding radical change. Fascism insists on political change, seeing that we cannot go on in this new interdependent world with the old national disunities, but that we must have some kind of new world order. Communism insists on economic change, seeing that the new technology forces on us new co-ordination in production and distribution. Democracy insists that we cannot continue plunging from one war into another, with conscriptions and regimentations multiplied until democracy itself will become impossible unless a co-operative world order stops these recurrent conflicts. These three—fascism, communism, and democracy—do radically differ, but one suspects that history, looking back, will say that the major fact in our time was that these three most powerful forces of our day were agreed on the necessity of radical change if a civilized world was to be possible. Well, when the three most powerful forces in the world call for change, we are going to get it. So intelligent minds are saying now that this is not simply another war—this is a revolution.

Who of us has not dreamed what it would be like to live in one of the world's stormy and tumultuous eras—the Reformation, the French Revolution, or what you will? They were fearful times but they were great times, too. Today no one need dream about that any more. We are now in the midst of the most revolutionary era in human history, with such momentous choices facing us as seldom have faced mankind before.

What makes any era seem great or little to a man is the man's own eyes, his capacity of insight and vision. Put some people in a great generation and they will only cry, "Who will show us any good?" But from Moses in the desert at the burning bush, seeing in an enslaved Israel in Egypt the hope of the future, to our own founding fathers, seeing in thirteen disunited colonies the possibility of a great venture in free living, men with eyes to see possibilities in times of travail and change have created the most hopeful advances in man's history. That is what we need to pray for now—eyes to see—for if we have them this will be for us a great time for great living.

We are not saying that the outcome of this war will necessarily be a constructive peace with a new and better era following. Upon the contrary, war is the most uncertain, the least precise instrument man handles. He picks it up to do something with it, and lo, when he is through he finds he has done something else altogether!

We fought the last war with two clear objectives in mind: First, to end the military threat of Germany. That end, however, we certainly did not achieve. We created Soviet Russia; we broke up the Hapsburg and Ottoman empires, trebled the size of Serbia, doubled the size of Rumania, created Iraq, Estonia, Lithuania, and Czechoslovakia. Such things, that we never intended to do, we did, but what we started out to do, conclusively to end Germany's military might, we did not do at all. Second, we fought the last war to make the world safe for democracy. Instead, we opened the door to one dictatorship after another—Kemal Ataturk in Turkey, Mussolini in Italy, Pilsudski in Poland, Salazar in Portugal, Franco in Spain, Hitler in Germany, but the one thing we started out to do, to make the world safe for democracy, we never did at all.

Always, world-changing conditions that we have not the slightest intention of producing come from war, while the aims and objectives we say we are fighting for are the very things it is least likely to achieve. Such is the essential nature of war. War is a blunderbuss with which one shoots at a bird and commonly hits everything in the vicinity except the bird.

Nevertheless, that is no excuse for us to cry, "Who will

show us any good?" It still remains true that the eras of enforced change present supreme opportunities. They challenge us with a sober and stimulating fact:

> We are living, we are dwelling
> In a grand and awful time,
> In an age on ages telling;
> To be living is sublime.

This is true not only because ours is an era calling for personal adequacy and forcing on us the necessity of momentous change, but an era also that reveals with unmistakable clarity the false reliances we have been trusting in.

. We have trusted in inventive science, and it is magnificent, but in the lurid light of this generation it is clear that what inventive science does is to furnish mankind with power, and that, far from solving the human problem, complicates it. The real question still rises: What moral quality shall exercise that power and to what end? There is no more scientifically competent nation on earth than Germany.

We have trusted in education, and its achievements have been splendid. Charlemagne towers as a great figure in history, but Charlemagne could neither read nor write. The spread of literacy, the invention of printing, the dispersion of books, the privilege of schools—all this is a thrilling story but it does not solve the problem. Education too is power, and still the question rises: What moral quality will use it and to what end? There is no more literate and educated nation on earth than Germany.

In such realms as these—inventive science and education —we commonly picture man's progress in terms of society's growing up from infancy to maturity. See, we say, our race has grown out of its primitive childhood! That is a true picture. We of the modern world have grown up and are not in our infancy any more. But is it not the grown-up people who cause all the trouble? It is not that little child who toddles about our home we are afraid of. We do not have to put him in prison or lock him up in an insane asylum. It is grown-up people for whom jails and asylums are built; it is maturity that suffers the appalling collapses. So society, when it is scientifically and educationally mature, can go berserk and insane, suffering such breakdowns as no primitive society ever knew. That is our problem—a society, growing scientifically and educationally mature, falling from one collapse into another.

This is a great time to be alive if only because it drives us back to the fundamentals: What shall it profit a man or a nation to gain the whole world and lose the soul? Many moderns have supposed that science and education were displacing the gospel and making it needless. Upon the contrary, the more mature society becomes, scientifically and educationally, the more critical is man's need of the principles of life, the sustaining faiths, the goals of endeavor, and the kind of character that Christ brought to the world. After the last war one of our popular artists drew a cartoon showing a group of men sitting down as a governmental cabinet to organize the new world. At the head of the table sat the President, and there too were the familiar portfolios, Secretary of War, Secretary of State, and all the rest, but a new figure was at that council table—there sat Christ with his portfolio, Secretary of Human Relationships. Until something like that happens I see no hope for the world. My fellow-Christians, for us especially this is a great time for great living now.

Finally, the greatness of our time lies in the fact that it not only calls thus for Christianity but challenges Christianity, too. We have said that scientific inventiveness and education cannot solve our problem. Yes, but there is plenty of Christianity that cannot solve our problem either—little, petty, hide-bound Christianity, an escape from life, utterly irrelevant to the vast issues that confront mankind.

In days like these one recalls that great Christianity has commonly emerged in troubled eras. We still go back to Saint

Augustine, that towering figure, across the centuries standing like a lighthouse in a stormy sea. When, then, did Augustine live and write his masterly *City of God* that is still one of the major events in Christian history? In the days when the Roman Empire fell and the whole earth was shaken. A great time calls for great religion.

If I were preaching today to fundamentalists, I would lay this heavily upon their consciences. All this Biblical literalism, this insistence on the peccadilloes of tradition, this sectarian provincialism in the church, this belated theology, is a travesty of what Christ's gospel ought to mean in such a day as this. I am speaking, however, not so much to fundamentalists as to liberals, and we too have sinned. For a long generation we have been engaged in simplifying the gospel, in saying to the intellectually perplexed, You need not believe this to be a Christian and you need not believe that. We have pared down the gospel, shrunk and reduced it until in our churches preachers have sometimes seemed to be playing a game to see how little a man can believe and still be a Christian.

Under no circumstances is that an adequate approach to religion. Science too has had to slough off old ideas and discard ancient superstitions. But science has not done it by shrinking the universe and making it simpler. It has enlarged the universe and made it more profound and vast than it ever was before. It has said not, See how little you have to think, but See how great a cosmos you live in and what immense vistas are open to your gaze!

So let Christianity speak in an era like this! Our problem is not to see how little we can believe but what great things we can see in the Christian message and make real to the world that desperately needs them. This is a great time for great convictions.

A prevalent mood, like a fog, settles down around us, in which we say, "Who will show us any good?" I have hoped that for some souls here we might bring in a northwest wind that would blow that fog away and give us a day of clearer seeing. This is a ghastly time to be alive—that is true, but not the whole truth. This is a great time also for spiritual adequacy, for wisdom and courage to face and create momentous change, for realistic appraisal of our false reliances, and for profound convictions about God and man and the kingdom of righteousness on earth. We are living

> In an age on ages telling;
> To be living is sublime.

Decisive Battles Behind Closed Doors

ONE advantage of knowing the Bible is that in days like
these one continually finds one's own experience there.
Reading it, one stops suddenly, saying, That is not
centuries ago but now, and that is not an ancient character
but myself. So one stops at the fifteenth verse of Jeremiah's
eighth chapter: "We looked for peace, but no good came; and
for a time of healing, and, behold, dismay!" That is ourselves,
disappointed and disillusioned, our lovely dreams of a peaceful world made safe for democracy become mirage.

Jeremiah was an idealist. In his early twenties he was called
to his prophethood in the springtime when the almond trees
blossomed, and eager for public reform, dreaming of a better
nation and a better world, he went out to follow the gleam.
He was one of those youths whom Lowell described,

> . . . with the rays
> Of morn on their white Shields of Expectation!

And now all his fine visions had deceived him. National and
international folly had brought ruin to his people; war was
upon them; the conqueror was at their very gates; dreadful
actualities mocked every dream that he had ever had. Who of
us now is not Jeremiah? As one of you said to me, "It is
not so much the awfulness of what is happening that gets me
down as it is the dismaying contrast between what is happening and all that we had dreamed."

War presents to sensitive minds two battlefields. They both
were present in Jeremiah's time—the outer battlefield where
the mighty hosts of Pharaoh-necoh, Nabopolazzar, and Nebuchadnezzar clashed with the hard-bestead forces of the Jews,
and that other battlefield, inside Jeremiah, where behind

closed doors he faced his spiritual struggle with disillusionment and cynicism. Both those battlefields were important,
but in the long perspective of history, which was more so?
Nebuchadnezzar won the outer war, and from that triumph
came vast immediate consequences, but Jeremiah won his
inner battle, too, and for forty years stood his ground, one of
the supreme seers of the race, and the results of that also
have been immense. The outer victory was like an earthquake
that changed the contour of the land; the inner victory was
like the development and scattering of seeds—vital, germinative seeds that grow and propagate themselves and live again,
century after century, so that when the earthquake is long
forgotten, they still clothe the land with verdure and feed the
people with their fruit. Out of Jeremiah's inner victory came
the great prophets of the Exile, and Christ, and the noblest
spiritual heritage that we possess. Here is one of the mysteries
of history, that battles fought behind closed doors in human
hearts, that make no noise, can be so much more enduring in
their results than the outer wars that shake the earth.

Again today both kinds of battlefield are here. No one
doubts the importance of the outer struggle. Its critical significance is daily dinned into our ears. But here in the church
our special business is with the other, and this at least is
true, that no outer triumph will bring any worth-while consequence unless in millions of human hearts a spiritual victory
is won over the kind of disillusionment that can get no further
than the lament, "We looked for peace, but no good came;
and for a time of healing, and, behold, dismay!"

To start with, Jeremiah was sorely tempted to give up the
faiths and hopes that he had trusted in. Had they not let him
down? Were they not mirages? Should he make a fool of
himself by trusting them again?

Who of us does not have moods when that temptation
surges in? All the theoretical arguments of the materialists
could not have persuaded us to give up Christian faith, but

now something more impressive than argument is here: terrific facts—the horror of man's brutality; the power of violence to shake to pieces, like an earthquake indeed, mankind's fragile gains of humaneness and decency. Is not Christ a visionary, and the Sermon on the Mount the ethic of a dreamer, and does not Christianity, making us softhearted, make us softheaded, too? That issue is being fought out on many an inner battlefield behind closed doors today.

Well, then, because of this appalling collapse of civilization that Christianity has not prevented, shall we give up our faith? If so, we cannot stop with surrendering Christianity. To be sure, Christ's gospel and ethic have not succeeded in preventing this catastrophe, but neither has education. That too has failed. If we begin surrendering to defeatism our faiths because they have not prevented this catastrophe, there is no place to stop. Nothing has prevented it—not Christianity, nor education, nor international law and statesmanship, nor democracy, nor the world-wide interdependencies of culture in music, art, and medicine. They all have failed. To discard them, however, because of that is as though a man, fallen into a pit, should saw off his own legs in despite because they had not prevented his falling in. On second thought he had better keep those legs—they are his only hope of ever climbing out again.

So, by the grace of God and common sense some of us will win this inner fight against disillusionment. Granted, that this war is the disgrace of Christianity! Granted, that the war's head and front are not in some unchristian land but in the heart of Europe where the church has had its deepest roots and its longest chance! Granted, that Christians should be stirred by shame and forced deeply to rethink their ways! Yet, when I for one go back to Christ and his basic teachings, never more profoundly did I believe in him than now. After this war and any other wars are over, with their ruin and disillusionment, Christ will be here—a lighthouse looking

[13]

down on ships that have wrecked themselves upon the reefs, but shining still upon the channel where deep water is. It is not Christ's gospel and ethic that have failed; it is the negation of them, their flouting and denial. People say today, What can we believe in—has not Christianity been tried and found wanting? Rather, the familiar saying is true that Christianity has not been tried and found wanting but found difficult and not tried.

Another factor must have entered into that inner struggle of Jeremiah, the temptation, namely, to be intimidated by the huge events of the outer world until the spiritual realities seemed weak and flimsy. Looked at in terms of the contemporary scene, how immense Nebuchadnezzar was, and how insignificant, Jeremiah. But how strangely different that scene looks now! Who was Nebuchadnezzar—no sooner victorious than his empire fell, and nothing left of him for ages, now, except a cruel name, a few clay tablets, and ruins where the jackals dwell? But in Jeremiah there was something that Nebuchadnezzar could not have understood nor guessed the issue of: ideas—vital, germinative ideas, invisible, intangible, spiritual, but with life in them.

Here is an aspect of history that in these days should come to our help—this amazing contrast, namely, between the transiency of size and the permanence of vitality. In the countryside we see its parable when a contest is staged between a great rock and a tiny seed. What chance has the seed against the rock? But live long enough, and we shall see how the seed's living tendrils will seek each vulnerable crevice out, will disintegrate with their vitality the very stone that stands against them until the living tree splits the great rock asunder. That is a true parable of history.

Today, if we let them, the huge events of our time will intimidate our souls. Size will make vitality seem feeble. But always the seeds of the future are the ideas that win their way inside the minds of men, and when those ideas are vital and germinative, they are mightier far than the hugest opposition that can withstand them.

> The great god Ra whose shrine once covered acres
> Is filler now for crossword puzzle makers.

The most decisive battles of history are always fought on the inner battlefield. Even in a war, behind the outer clash of armies is the quiet debate in the councils of the strategists. Behind the lawyer's stirring plea, winning his case in public court, are his unseen decisions in his private thinking. "Cases," so runs the legal proverb, "are won in chambers." Behind a great career that moves the world are inner struggles that make no noise. Behind the character of Christ is a chamber with the door shut, where the soul prays. And there on that inner battlefield—where every one of us must fight today, inexorably drafted for *that* war—the long-term issues of our generation will be decided.

Even the Nazis know that. As Jesus said, children of darkness are often wiser in their generation than the children of light. What is the most dreadful thing that has gone on in the lands conquered by the Nazis? Not, I think, the outward loss of liberty, the shooting of hostages, the starvation of bodies, nor all the despair of political subjugation, terrible as they are. The most dreadful thing is the Nazi policy of capturing the minds of the people, shutting up schools that will not teach Nazi doctrine, forcing children away from their homes and churches, and perverting education, so that from infancy up they may be drilled in Nazi ways of thought, until, as one German woman who fled nazidom wrote, "The best that grew in the land was being torn out by the roots because the children had been taught to regard it as weeds." The Nazis have read history to good purpose. They know how transient military victory by itself alone has always been, and so, on a scale never proposed before by any conqueror, they make military victory only a prelude to the real victory that alone can last, the conquest of the thinking of the people. Even they know that in the long run the question whether any regime can endure will be decided on that inner battlefield.

One thinks with admiration of souls in Europe today standing like Jeremiah over against Nebuchadnezzar. If that is important in Europe, it is important here. Our minds still are our own, and it makes a difference to all the world who wins the inner battle there: faith or cynicism, cowardice or courage, Christ or antichrist!

Jeremiah's struggle, however, was not alone the temptation to surrender his great faiths and to let the gigantic events of his time bulldoze his soul and make spiritual realities seem feeble. All this came to its climax in the sense of personal strain. He had been so confident an idealist. He had counted on the reforms of Josiah to save his nation, much as some of us counted on the League of Nations, and now it all had flopped. His problem was intimate and emotional—the personal strain was too much.

A few weeks ago I visited my old college campus, and thought of the days long ago when first I came as a lad to that college town. We were then in the full tide of nineteenth century liberalism. We took democracy for granted and its universal spread as predestined. We were Tennysonian optimists:

> I doubt not thro' the ages an increasing purpose runs,
> And the thoughts of men are widen'd with the process of
> of the suns.

We were disciples of Browning:

> God's in his heaven—
> All's right with the world!

And now, an older and soberer man, I walked that campus feeling on every side the pressure of the Second World War in one lifetime and seeing in every lad I passed potential cannon fodder. That situation poses for all my generation more than a theoretical problem to be met by argument: it presents an emotional problem of stress and strain.

This sense of letdown and disillusionment is intensified when we recall the high hopes that filled the two decades after the First World War. The outspoken hatred of war is old, from Euripides in Greece, and Isaiah and Jeremiah in Israel, but never before has there been such a rising tide of revulsion against it as in our day, between the two wars. In best-selling novels and in the theater before applauding audiences, war was pictured in all its stark horror. We renounced war as individuals; and as nations too in the Kellogg-Briand Pact. Scientists spoke out about the effects of war as they never had spoken before, like Professor Earnest A. Hooton, the Harvard anthropologist, saying, "Armed conflict kills and cripples the best and the most vigorous of the breeding stock and wreaks havoc upon the nervous or endocrine organization of potential mothers, thereby lowering the quality of the offspring they produce. It depresses nutritional and general environmental conditions so that a postwar generation is conceived in pathology and born in despair." Dr. Nicholas Murray Butler estimated that the First World War cost thirty million lives and four hundred billion dollars, and he figured that with that amount we could have placed a twenty-five hundred dollar house, with a thousand dollars worth of furniture, on five acres of land, for every family in the United States, Canada, Australia, England, Wales, Ireland, Scotland, France, Belgium, Germany, and Russia, with enough left over to give to every city of twenty thousand inhabitants or more in all those countries a five million dollar library and a ten million dollar university. As for religious leaders, what did they not say against war and in favor of peace? Shakespeare's words in *King Henry V* took on new meaning in our minds:

> . . . the flesh'd soldier, rough and hard of heart,
> In liberty of bloody hand shall range
> With conscience wide as hell, mowing like grass
> Your fresh-fair virgins and your flowering infants.

So we said we would have no more to do with war, but now it is here again, and what would Shakespeare say today about it with "conscience wide as hell" mowing down the innocent?

It is easy to say that we ought to confront this situation as a challenge and rise to meet it. Of course we ought! Raoul de Roussy de Sales, in his book, *The Making of Tomorrow*, is right, however: "If the war is long, it will be harder for the Americans to maintain their standard of thinking than their standard of living." Maintaining a high standard of living in this country is a public problem, but after all, millions of us could endure a far lower standard of living without its hurting us one bit, and we will doubtless have to. But to maintain through a disillusioning time like this a high standard of thinking is a private problem. One wishes one could shout from the housetops to all America: a lower standard of living may well be necessary, but do not lower your standard of thinking!

One of the finest things ever said about anyone was said about Robert E. Lee by his biographer, Douglas Freeman. For over ten years, as he wrote that great biography, Freeman lived, as it were, with Lee. He rose, and ate, and thought, and felt, and slept with Lee, and at the end he said of those laborious years, "I have been fully repaid by being privileged to live, . . . for more than a decade in the company of a great gentleman." So! To go through the disappointments and disillusionments that Lee went through, and still, in poise and kindliness, in wisdom, and in magnanimity even toward his enemies, to remain a great gentleman, not to surrender, to the horror of a violent era and the mass degeneration of wartime propaganda, the inner decencies of the spirit and the farseeing wisdom of magnanimity—that was maintaining a high standard of thinking when it was hard. Of course, we ought to do that!

For myself, however, I can do that only if I see clearly that this present view of life now forced upon us, this soberer outlook on mankind's problem, is far truer than that old nineteenth century's easy-going liberal optimism that was so pleasant but so false. Don't give up your great faiths, we have said, but that does not mean going back to the fool's paradise of confidence in inevitable progress, as though democracy necessarily would spread and peace automatically arrive. I too feel the dreadful emotional strain of these days, but I see something deeper happening here. We are looking now straight at some truths that in our palmy days of easy optimism we never saw. Democracy is not inevitable, but is a long-drawn-out cause demanding all the intelligence, devotion, and character we are capable of. Peace is not a mere logical deduction from new world interdependencies, but the most difficult task that mankind ever undertook, the way to it blockaded by huge obstacles both in outer circumstance and in the deep-seated prejudice and greed of human hearts. In this more serious view we are seeing realities that make nostalgia for the old days of easy optimism a shameful thing. Democracy and peace are not goals to be ridden to on a toboggan moved by resistless gravitation, but are long-term causes to be served by us and by our children against innumerable difficulties. That soberer insight is more true, more stimulating, yes, more hopeful than our old superficial optimism ever was, for there was no hope in that.

So today, if we are wise, we are neither easy-going optimists nor yet discouraged cynics, but realists, knowing that we are up against the most complicated and difficult problem mankind ever faced, trusting no panaceas, expecting no easy outcomes, but no defeatists either about democracy or Christianity or ultimate world organization and peace. There is hope in that soberer attitude.

Well, that was Jeremiah's experience. He never was again his former youthful, too-sanguine self, expecting easy remedies to heal the world's deep ills, but he was immeasurably a bigger man, and at the heart of that inner victory was his unconquerable faith that because God is, spiritual vitality is always stronger than size. Ah, Nebuchadnezzar, you thought you were up against the armies of Israel only, and you laughed at them. You were up against something mightier than that, something in the soul of man—the love of liberty, the sense of human dignity, faith in God—that had behind it the Eternal Purpose, and that outlasted your transient triumph as stars outlast a tallow dip. That one man, Jeremiah, whom you scarcely noticed, was mightier far and more enduring than you and all your empire could ever be. So still the living trees will split the great rocks, and the living seeds clothe the landscapes that forgotten earthquakes changed.

Righteousness First!*

MANY people picture Jesus as an idealist, exclusively interested in man's spiritual well-being. He came into the world, they think, to save souls. As the Gospels present him, however, the Master, far from being interested only in men's souls, was immensely concerned about their day-by-day, practical, mundane needs. He spent a large part of his time healing sick bodies. His test at the final judgment was whether we had fed the hungry, given drink to the thirsty, and clothed the naked. The sight of a rich man in luxury while a poor man lay untended at the gate was to him intolerable. Everywhere in the Gospels Jesus is presented as wanting us to have what we naturally want to have—physical well-being, economic security, food, clothes, health.

This fact about Jesus has been obscured by a type of other-worldly spirituality trying to be more spiritual than the Master himself, until many miss the meaning in one of the greatest passages in the Sermon on the Mount. Jesus, talking about what we shall eat and what we shall drink and wherewithal we shall be clothed, tells his disciples not to let anxiety about such matters master them, and, reading the passage, many stop with that emphasis, supposing that Jesus means that such things are not important enough to worry over; concerning which idea we feel that that attitude may be conceivable for a saint but not for us. Upon the contrary, finish the passage and see that instead of minimizing these natural wants Jesus is telling us how to fulfill them. Far from saying that the basic necessities of life are not important, what the Master really says is this: "Your heavenly Father knoweth that ye have need of all these things. But seek ye first his kingdom, and

* Preached February 20, 1944.

[21]

his righteousness; and all these things shall be added unto you."

So that is what Jesus is driving at; not that our basic human wants—the welfare of our bodies, the security of our families, the prosperity of our economy, the safety of our nation—are unimportant, but that we will never get these great boons without fulfilling a prior condition: righteousness first!

So familiar is this verse that it commonly slips off our minds like water from a slate roof, yet what a tremendous statement it is! Here we human beings are, wanting the good things of life and trying to get them by anxiously pouncing on them like leopards, saying, I want what I want when I want it; and Jesus says, You ought to want such things but you will never enduringly get them until you fulfill a prior condition: righteousness first; then, and only then, shall these things be added unto you.

That statement sounds not so much like a visionary proclaiming an ideal as like a scientist announcing a law. Countless things men for centuries wanted and vainly strove for, and then at last science, discovering some basic, underlying truth about the universe and its laws, said, Put this first, and all these things shall be added unto you—light for your houses, power for your industries, cure for your diseases. Jesus' statement belongs in that category. It is no visionary ideal but an everlasting law, without whose fulfillment mankind will never get the things that most it wants: righteousness first!

Suppose that even on this Sunday of patriotic import, between the birthdays of our national heroes, I should ring the changes on the slogan, "America First." Everybody here would wince. There always was something the matter with that slogan, "America First." Are we not, then, patriots? Do we not want America to be great in power, prosperity, and leadership? Of course, we want it, but even in this realm Jesus' statement holds good: We cannot get what we want for America if we put America first; we must put something else first: righteousness first, a decent world order, an established reign of law among all nations, mankind organized for justice and peace. *That* we must put first, or alas, America will fall from one disaster to another.

Here is a basic law upon whose recognition all good fortune everywhere depends. Day after day in this church joyous couples, newly wedded, with high anticipation launch new homes concerning which they cherish hopes of life-long happiness. Watching them across the years, however, one sees the inexorable operation of this truth that Jesus stated. The things they want, they ought to want—security and peace, happy children, and lovely memories accumulating with the years. The Master would say to them again, "Your heavenly Father knoweth that ye have need of all these things." But what wreckage can come to homes that forget the rest of what he said! The ultimate foundations of a great home are ethical. Romance can start a home but romance alone cannot sustain one—only fidelity can maintain a fine family. One wishes that before it is too late all newly-weds could see that: put righteousness first—fidelity, trustworthiness, fair play—only then is there some good chance that all these other things shall be added unto us.

On this Sunday, therefore, full of concern for, and loyalty to, our nation, I speak to you about some things we want that we will never get except by the route the Master pointed out: righteousness first.

For one thing, we want a great nation that will preserve unspoiled and carry to new meaning its heritage of liberty and democracy. Now, however, in a war fought, we say, on behalf of liberty and democracy, we find ourselves in danger of losing within our own borders the very things we fight for. For modern war is essentially totalitarian. It forces us toward dictatorship. It has to be waged with an ever increasing concentration of power in the government's hands.

Ever since Hitler rose to the ascendancy in Germany he

has been preparing for war. How did he go about it? Say your worst about him, he understands how to wage modern war; so he began by scrapping democracy and establishing a dictatorship. He knows the basic requirement of total war, and every nation that wages war today must in some degree imitate him.

As this year, therefore, we keep the birthdays of our national heroes, a profound anxiety burdens all thoughtful people in this nation. The priceless heritage of our founding fathers has our undying loyalty. We would give our lives for it. We want what they wanted—that government "of the people, by the people, for the people, shall not perish from the earth." But it becomes ever more clear that achieving that involves more than the military defeat of Hitler; it involves the defeat of what he stands for, of his philosophy, and above all it involves the abolition of war, which is the incarnation of his philosophy and which itself creates dictatorship in every nation that wages it.

I am not in particular criticizing our present administration when I call your attention to the fact that Congress has been passing on an average about thirteen hundred new laws a year, that some two hundred government bureaus without law-making powers under the Constitution are promulgating rules and regulations of their own, and that we are being regimented and conscripted and dictated to in ways that would make our founding fathers turn over in their graves. That kind of thing is always involved in modern war. In war we find ourselves in a position where we want the government to do things for us that only the government can do, but then, when we have given the government power to do things for us, we wake up to find that the government has power to do things to us. So Thomas Jefferson once asked, "What has destroyed liberty and the rights of man in every government which has ever existed under the sun?" And he answered, "The generalizing and concentrating all cares and powers into one body."

We have called Christ an idealist too long. He is not so much an idealist as a revealer of everlasting laws. We deeply want liberty and democracy in this country, but if we are to keep them we must put something else first: God's Kingdom and his righteousness. Unless we can establish first a just and durable world order, good for all mankind, we shall not ourselves be able to keep democracy but will drift and drift, as we are drifting now, through one war after another toward dictatorship. I wonder if Major-General O'Ryan, of the American Expeditionary Force in France in the last war, was thinking of this when he said: "I would be a traitor to my country if I did not do everything in my power to abolish war."

If, therefore, we Americans have any real care for democracy, isolationism is out, and we must go as far as we can toward a just world order. That first! In the Constitutional Convention that made of our thirteen dissevered colonies one nation, George Washington said very little. One day, however, he rose and made a brief but immortal speech: "It is too probable that no plan we propose will be adopted. Perhaps another dreadful conflict is to be sustained. If to please the people, we offer what we ourselves disapprove, how can we afterwards defend our work? Let us raise a standard to which the wise and honest can repair. The event is in the hand of God."

That attitude is deeply needed now. We fully count on winning the war, but only a blind man can be optimistic about winning the peace: "It is too probable that no plan we propose will be adopted. Perhaps another dreadful conflict is to be sustained." So, in one of the most critical hours in human history Washington speaks again: If we really want liberty and democracy, "Let us raise a standard to which the wise and honest can repair. The event is in the hand of God."

For another thing, we deeply want for ourselves and our children a world where the magnificent new powers that science gives us will be used to create a more abundant life and not destroy it. One of our church families received recently a letter from one of our boys just starting overseas. Here are a few sentences from it: "I treasure memories of the good old days . . . when I conjured up pictures of myself as doing something truly creative. . . . The very word 'creative' was like a goal to me. . . . How vividly I remember when I became a member of Riverside Church and Dr. Fosdick asked what I planned to do after college. It was with the utmost assurance I answered, 'Something creative.' I wonder what he would think of me now, catapulted out of college into something truly DESTRUCTIVE, dealing with the most treacherous and insidious agents conceivable."

What I think of that boy in affection and prayerful good wishes, and in penitent shame, too, that we, the older generation, ever let this happen to him, would not go into words. He is facing in his own life the major problem that the world faces. He wanted to do something creative with the splendid new powers that modern knowledge puts within our grasp, and now he finds himself compelled to use them not for creation but for destruction.

We older people grew up in a generation whose major slogan might be phrased thus: Seek ye first science and its powers, and all these things shall be added unto you. How reasonable that sounded! What vistas opened up before mankind as one realm of power after another came under our control! But now Jesus again proves to be right. Something else must be put first—righteousness first—or else all these powers laid hold on by demonic forces, twisted to diabolical ends, will destroy the life and culture, the art and beauty, the homes, economies, and cities of men on a scale hitherto undreamed. The most terrifying fact about our modern world is the scientific power we have with which to destroy ourselves.

Did you see that recent cartoon: two cell mates in prison talking together, and one says proudly to the other: "I'm going to study and improve myself, and when you're still a common thief I'll be an embezzler"? There, alas, is a picture of our modern world, where new knowledge only increases our capacity for more extensive ruination.

As we leave the church today we shall sing one of our patriotic hymns, written in the optimistic era in which we elders were reared. It is a grand hymn and we shall sing it with full hearts, yet when one comes to lines like

> O beautiful for patriot dream
> That sees beyond the years
> Thine alabaster cities gleam,
> Undimmed by human tears,

I should think there would be a catch in our throats. This modern world's alabaster cities undimmed by human tears! It does not look like that, and the more scientific power we get, the less it looks like that, unless—everything hangs on that "unless"—unless we put God's Kingdom and his righteousness first.

If I believed in God for no other reason, I would believe in him because this law that Jesus stated is so everlastingly true. Can you imagine a world as the materialists picture it—nothing ultimately real here except protons and electrons going it blind—with a law like this built into the structure of the cosmos: that no good thing men want can be obtained unless they put righteousness first? That is no reasonable characteristic of a materialistic universe. That kind of quality belongs only in a world where there is a God of moral law, so that all that endures must be built upon his immutable foundations of ethical righteousness.

Yet, cosmic though this truth is in its implications, and applicable particularly to our nation as a whole, let us not miss its individual import! Putting righteousness first is always, at bottom, a personal affair. If the nation and the world ever do it, it will be because enough individuals have done it. When the church today calls for a renewal of spiritual life, for men and women one by one transformed by the renewing of their minds, its plea can hardly be heard amid the thundering violence of a warring world, and yet without that spiritual renewal there is no hope. As Confucius said, "It is not square acres which make a country great, but square men."

When in these days we think of the critical necessity of a world organized for mutual protection and the maintenance of international justice and peace, we think in terms of politics. There must be a new political organization of the world to represent the international interests of mankind, we say, and we are right. But all great structures require two things. First, the wisdom of the architects, planning how the structure may be put together well, and second, the raw material, strong and durable enough to build the structure of. Well, we, one by one, are the raw material of any world order that ever can be built. My soul, seek first God's Kingdom and his righteousness!

On this day of patriotic import with so many men and women here in uniform I should not wish to end our sermon without a further emphasis. Another thing we want is a world that will not disappoint the hopes of our youths who are pouring out their lives for us.

American youths have not been trained in a military tradition, and seeing war now at firsthand they loathe it. One of our members in the South Seas recently wrote: "War is still the most wasteful and hateful thing that I know of; no one really gains anything by it in the long run." As for the sustaining hope that keeps them going through the dreadful days, it is the faith that somehow because of their sacrifice their children can be spared another holocaust like this. So one of our boys in a recent letter said: "One thought keeps on going through my mind, that some day there will emerge, created out of all the misery, a *kinder* humanity. Too intangible,

[28]

utterly unpredictable, perhaps, but not impossible, and a thought of this kind inspires one to carry on."

We talk all the time about backing these boys up, but are we going to back them up in the thing that the best of them are most hoping for? They will win the war—at what a cost!—but we along with them must win the peace, and at that point we run again into the everlasting truth of Jesus' law: we cannot put party first, or economic self-interest first, or absolute national sovereignty first, or imperialistic greed first, or racial prejudice first. If we do we shall be rightly damned forever in the estimation of our offspring. We must put righteousness first.

In the midst of the last war Mr. H. G. Wells wrote some terrifying sentences so prophetic that I wish they could be engraved now on the consciences of all of us!

Mars will sit like a giant above all human affairs for the next two decades and the speech of Mars is blunt and plain. He will say to us all: "Get your houses in order. If you squabble among yourselves, waste time, litigate, muddle, snatch profits and shirk obligations, I will certainly come down upon you again. I have taken all your men between eighteen and fifty, and killed and maimed such as I pleased; millions of them. I have wasted your substance—contemptuously. Now, mark you, you have multitudes of male children between the ages of nine and nineteen running about among you. Delightful and beloved boys. And behind them come millions of delightful babies. Of these I have scarcely smashed and starved a paltry hundred thousand perhaps by the way. But go on muddling, each for himself and his parish and his family and none for all the world, go on in the old way, stick to your 'rights,' stick to your 'claims,' each one of you, make no concessions and no sacrifices, obstruct, waste, squabble, and presently I will come back again and take all that fresh harvest of life I have spared, all those millions that are now sweet children and dear little boys and youths, and I will squeeze it into red pulp between my hands, I will mix it with the mud of trenches and feast on it before your eyes, even more damnably than I have done with your grown-up sons and young men. And I have taken most of your superfluities already; next time I will take your barest necessities."

Well, that has come to pass, and if it is not to come to pass again, righteousness first!

Ah, America, our loyalty is yours. As in our fathers' days our lives, our fortunes, and our sacred honor are committed to you. But just because we love you, God help us to see that all the good fortune we want for you depends upon a prior condition: "Seek ye first the kingdom of God, and his righteousness; and all these things shall be added unto you."

The Field Is the World

ONE of the most fascinating aspects of history is the way ideas that at first seemed incredibly idealistic have turned out in the end to be overwhelmingly realistic, and seldom has that happened more clearly than in the case of Jesus' words: "The field is the world." When first he said that it must have seemed a wild idea—that young teacher from Nazareth telling his slender band of disciples that the scope of their work was the world. Today, however, that statement has become a realistic, austere fact that we cannot anyhow escape, concerning which only God knows whether we are going to be able to handle it. "The field is the world."

When Christians first took that statement in earnest, it meant simply that they should go as missionaries to the ends of the earth. It means that still. Here is a letter written by one of our American soldiers on a South Sea island to his pastor, Father Flanagan, at home. Last Thanksgiving Day, he says, the natives of the island, hearing of our American holiday, prepared a celebration of it for our men—a native dance, and the children singing—and the boy writes this:

> We then witnessed something that I do not believe will ever leave our memory. The chief arose and spoke to his people for about ten minutes. He spoke in his native tongue. I understand a little of the language and knew he was giving them a sermon. I later found out though that he had quoted several verses of the Bible by memory. He then faced the soldiers and picked up his Bible and read the same passages in English. I was utterly astounded afterwards when I looked at his Bible—it was in his native tongue and he had translated it as he read along without faltering once. He then led us in a prayer of thanksgiving to close the program.

I looked around and tried to observe just what was the reaction of the men. I don't think there was a one of us who didn't feel real love and admiration for that black boy. I don't suppose a group of whites have ever before been led in prayer by a man who is generally believed to be ignorant or termed savage. But a few short years ago his people were headhunters and cannibals.

When we look at the simple life and the love of God these natives display, it makes you wonder just which race is ignorant or savage.

That is moving testimony to the reality of the missionary's work, taking in earnest that "the field is the world," but who does not see that that very scene on a South Sea island, with our sons there on a mission of violence and death, says something more than that? It says that these words of the Master have now taken on a new meaning. We cannot go on simply sending emissaries of the gospel to the ends of the earth; we must somehow organize the earth so that generation after generation we do not negative their work and deny their gospel by sending Christendom's armies and navies to fight at the ends of the earth. The idea that the field is the world has now taken on a vast political significance—the central concern of the world's statesmen—in which the Christian church has an immense stake. The world must now be organized as a co-operative community, or we are sunk. The gist of our sermon, then, is this: The international organization of mankind, while it is a political task, is nonetheless the Christian church's concern, the contemporary, realistic application of a conviction, without which Christianity is not Christianity at all: "The field is the world."

Consider first the fact that in this country we cannot possibly be isolationist even if we want to. Certainly, we ought by this time to have learned that we cannot be isolationist when war comes. If ever a whole people wanted to stay out of war, we wanted to stay out of this one. Already a legend is growing up to the general effect that it was only a can-

tankerous minority—"America First," and such groups—
that tried to keep us out of war, but that misrepresents the
facts. Late in 1939, shortly after the outbreak of war in
Europe, *Fortune* magazine conducted a survey whose result
was that while 83.1 per cent of our people were on the side
of the Allies, only 3.3 per cent were willing to go to war, and
only 13.5 per cent would fight even if the Allies were losing.
At that time President Roosevelt said, "Let no man or
woman thoughtlessly or falsely talk of America sending its
armies to European fields. . . . I hope the United States will
keep out of this war. I believe that it will." In July, 1940,
President Roosevelt said, "We will not send our men to take
part in European wars"; in November, 1940, President
Roosevelt said in a Brooklyn address, "I am fighting to keep
our people out of foreign wars"; and again, in a Cleveland
address, "The first purpose of our foreign policy is to keep
our country out of war." In such statements the President
had the overwhelming mass of our citizens behind him. Twice
now by every device we could turn our wits to we have tried
to be isolationist in a global war, and it cannot be done. How
long are we going on with this insane policy of being, perforce,
interventionist in war, and still trying to be isolationist in
peace?

If someone says, But why beat a dead lion—for isolationism
is now a dead issue—I answer, Among intelligent people of
course it is a dead issue; but emotionally it is not dead, and
when the fighting stops we shall confront such an emotional
reaction—such homesickness for normalcy, along with such
difficulties, sacrifices, compromises, disillusionments, and indignation, in trying to work together with Russia, the British
Empire and all the rest—that the temptation to give it up,
come back home and tuck ourselves into bed here will be
tremendous.

Let us then say to ourselves now—and try to remember it
when that emotional reaction sets in—that no such thing as

[33]

isolation is possible for the United States under any circumstances. The post-war world will be organized one way or another; the United States cannot possibly stay out, and the only question is: to which of three general types will that post-war organization of the world belong? The balance-of-power system—that is one. Some say that that is all this war will issue in—a new balance-of-power system. Well, if the post-war world is going to be organized thus, we shall be in that up to our necks—we cannot be isolated from that. The second possible type of post-war organization General Patton described the other day—Great Britain, Russia, and the United States ruling the world. That is a conceivable plan, but the indignant public response to General Patton's statement reveals our instinctive awareness of the fact that to have three powerful nations set out to rule the world offers no possible hope of permanency, no conceivable chance of bringing ultimate peace. As for the United States under that plan, we would be in it over our heads—there is no isolationism in that. So we face the third possible plan—a global organization that in the end will take all nations in, a genuine endeavor to deal with international problems by international political instruments, making the welfare of all the concern of each, and the welfare of each the responsibility of all. Difficult? Of course it is difficult, sometimes seeming too good to be possible, so that even those who believe in it, like Professor Mortimer Adler, say that while it will surely come in the end, it may take five hundred years to reach it. But the fact remains that we have only three choices for the post-war world: balance-of-power system; a triumvirate ruling the world; an inclusive organization of all nations—these three, and no others—and in none of them is American isolationism a possibility.

So for us "the field is the world," and in the choice we make now between those three plans of world organization the church of Christ has a stake so great that Christ himself will be crucified again if we take the wrong road.

The second consideration I ask you to think about is this: we deeply need now—not later, but now—a clear policy concerning which choice we are going to make. President Roosevelt himself has said, "Winning the war will be futile if we do not throughout the period of its winning keep our people prepared to make a lasting and worthy peace." We hear that among the men in the camps and at the front the question is commonly discussed as to what we are fighting for. Certain immediate answers to that question are obvious. To defeat the military parties in Germany and Japan and to free ourselves from the fear of their aggression—that is clear. But that kind of answer is not enough now. When Hitler and his allies are defeated, what then?

Listen to the popular debate now going on in this country concerning the terms of peace and see the danger we are in! The criteria used in that popular debate are mainly emotional. One group in this city met and after a long discussion as to the adjective to be applied to the kind of peace they desired, they decided on "generous." They want a generous peace. But the followers of Vansittart and such like want a stern, punitive, Carthaginian peace. Am I wrong in thinking that this debate over emotional criteria gets us nowhere? Generous peace—what does that mean? Stern, punitive peace— what does that mean? Such adjectives are emotional. They spring out of sentimentality on one side or vindictiveness on the other. Were I to choose an adjective I should say that I want a hardheaded peace, by which I mean terms of peace that start with a clearly visualized idea of what we want to accomplish, and then intelligently, objectively—if you will, scientifically—adapt whatever we do to Germany and Japan to the achieving of that aim. Got at in that way some of the factors in the peace will be stern, punitive, and some will be generous, magnanimous, constructive, but the criterion of decision will be neither softness and leniency on the one side, nor severity and sternness on the other. The criterion will be our dominant aim to build a world organization that can ultimately take all nations in.

The biggest question now before us about the post-war world is: what do we really want? Do we really want a society of nations that has in it some fair chance of saving our children from global war? Well, then, if we want that, let us rid ourselves of all the emotionalism we can—sentimentality on one side, and vengefulness and hatred on the other—and make of that endeavor a hardheaded, scientific proposition, adapting our means intelligently to that end.

As between the two emotional dangers—sentimentality on one side and vengefulness on the other—the greater popular peril, I suspect, comes from the latter mood: anger, hatred, vindictiveness. That is doubtless why Mr. Herbert Hoover said: "We can have revenge or we can have peace, but we cannot have both." Hardheaded students of public affairs are saying that some of the plans proposed for the post-war treatment of Germany have no discoverable relationship with an endeavor to build a real society of nations. Such proposals as the complete destruction of Germany, its dismemberment and its permanent policing by the Allied nations are naturally born out of the turbulent emotions of war, but see the stern facts they run headlong into! For one thing, the fact that the world's prosperity is indivisible, and that a prosperous world cannot be achieved with a permanently crushed and ruined Germany at the heart of Europe. For another thing, the fact that while the destruction of the military party in Germany is an absolute necessity, and stern measures also to prevent its return to power, when punitive action is extended to the children, born and unborn, presenting them as they come on with a hopeless situation and outlook, we are sowing the seeds of a revolt that will convulse the world. Remember Shakespeare's words:

> Heat not a furnace for your foe so hot
> That it do singe yourself.

For another thing, the fact that we of the Western world, we Britishers and Americans, for example, are too civilized to go on enforcing a Carthaginian peace like that, fifteen or twenty years from now. We will not do it. All our history demonstrates that we will not do it. So a hardheaded peace involves both elements—sternness and severity, to be sure, but underneath that and determining all the means we use, constructive, intelligent goodwill, motivated by a dominant aim to achieve a world organization that ultimately will take all nations in.

This means political action backed by powerful public opinion. At this point we Christians need to be on our guard for we are tempted to be individualists, thinking that if only enough good people in the world hate war and love peace, that will assure peace. But millions upon millions of individuals hating war and loving peace will not assure peace. There are such millions now. The great mass of the common folk of the world feel that way now, and yet look at us in the thick of a war that overpasses in horror and destructiveness anything hitherto seen on earth. No! If all the individuals in the world hated war and loved peace, that would not assure peace. Peace is now a political problem of world organization.

Look at Europe, for example, where these world wars start! West of Russia, before this war, there was in Europe an area two-thirds the size of the United States, politically split up into twenty-six separate national sovereignties, with their customs barriers, tariffs, currencies, military establishments, with their natural rivalries accentuated by political separation, and with no common, unified governmental agency to represent their mutual concerns. In these days of interdependence, if Europe were inhabited by saints, they could not manage with such a political structure the peaceful handling of their real and vital interests.

On November 10, 1918, Adolf Hitler, a war casualty, was in a German hospital. He was, as he describes himself, "a nameless man in an army of eight million." The hospital chaplain broke the news to him that all was over—the war lost and the surrender made. In *Mein Kampf* Hitler describes the agony with which he greeted that first Armistice Day: "I groped my way back to the dormitory, threw myself on my cot and buried my burning head in the covers and pillows." But listen to the sentence with which that passage ends: "I resolved," said Hitler, "I resolved now to become a politician."

That was a fateful day in human history when one man who hated peace and wanted war resolved to become a politician, and that kind of resolve can be met by nothing less than millions of people who love peace and hate war, resolving to be politicians too. This world is going to be politically organized, one way or another, either under an imposed totalitarianism or under a just and freely chosen system of co-operation.

We often celebrate the Declaration of Independence as the beginning of our nation, but our forefathers could have issued declarations of independence by the dozen and still we might never have been a nation. After the Declaration of Independence came something else, more prosaic, essentially political —a group of men gathered in Philadelphia and sitting down to write the Constitution. It was the Constitution that made us a nation. In our endeavors after peace we are at that stage now. On the question of war our declaration of independence has been made—we do hate war and want peace. But now everything depends on a world constitution that will make peace a practical possibility. Millions of us must say, each in his or her own way, I resolve now to be a politician.

The third consideration naturally follows. We, the people, need to face now the price that such a real community of nations is going to cost, and we need to make up our minds that it is worth whatever it may cost.

Lincoln Steffens tells us that at one stage in the proceedings at the Versailles conference Clemenceau turned on Woodrow Wilson, Orlando, and Lloyd George, and asked them bluntly whether they really meant what they said about wanting "permanent peace." They all declared they did mean it. Then Clemenceau specified some of the sacrifices that would be involved—the surrender of imperialism, the tearing down of tariff walls, the adjustment of economic inequalities and the removal of restrictions on immigration, upon which the others protested that they did not have that in mind. "Then," said Clemenceau, "you don't mean peace. You mean war." And Lincoln Steffens adds this comment of his own: "Wilson did not want peace, not literally; nor do we Americans, nor do the British, mean peace. We do not want war; nobody in the world wants war; but some of us do want the things we can't have without war."

That is the nub of the whole business as it will confront us when this conflict is over—not wanting war, but not willing, either, to pay the price of peace. One's heart grows sick to see many Americans today shy off from the only constructive endeavor that can possibly bring peace because they see national sovereignty invaded, or economic sacrifice demanded, or even racial prejudice disregarded.

We have our choice. We will pay the price of peace or else in a few years we will pay again the price of war. From that dilemma there is no escape—it is one or the other. And when one balances the cost of peace against the cost of war how can one be unwilling to pay the first?

Take one look, I beg of you, at the cost of war. Its economic cost, loading on us a debt we will stagger under for generations—and in comparison with that what are all the economic sacrifices we will ever make to maintain a real society of nations? The governmental cost of war, threatening us even in this country with a dictatorial bureaucracy that frightens everyone among us who has the tradition of American freedom in his heart—and in comparison with that what is the cost in qualified national sovereignty that peace will ever require? The human cost of war—nine million prisoners of war behind barbed wire this Sunday morning, millions more doomed to death by epidemics, starvation, and the bloody processes of war itself—what are all the costs of peace compared with that?

I see here many men in uniform, and I know I speak for them and for their comrades. They are ready to lay down their lives, but if that must be, they want to lay them down for something worth dying for, and they know that in the long run, whether or not that objective worth dying for will be achieved depends not only on the outcome of the war, but on what we, the great mass of the citizens, do afterward. When war stops, tired with the long strain, shall we let up, relax, say, Why worry now? and as we did the last time plunge into a decade of individual and national self-seeking? Shall we be beguiled again by those who promise a return to normalcy? President Harding, who won his election promising that he would lead us back to normalcy, stood at the tomb of the Unknown Soldier on November 11, 1921, and said, "This Armistice Day shall mark the beginning of a new and lasting era of peace on earth." Lovely words! But in all history was there ever a clearer illustration of crying, Peace, peace; when there was no peace? If after this war we so betray the sacrifices of our youth again, we shall be contemptible indeed.

A real society of nations is worth whatever it may cost. Even when we have done our best I am not too hopeful. Optimism is silly in the face of the difficulties we confront. The obstacles are immense and tragic. Remember in the film *Madame Curie*, that after the 487th experiment had failed Pierre gives up in despair, crying, "It can't be done; it can't be done! Maybe in a hundred years it can be done but never in our lifetime," and Madame Curie confronts him with resolute face, saying, "If it takes a hundred years it will be a pity, but I dare not do less than work for it so long as I have life." Some such determination must be ours if we are to win on this great issue.

Boulder Dam is a notable engineering feat, and like all worth-while achievements it cost sacrifice. Eighty-nine men lost their lives in building it, but they at least knew that what they died for would be accomplished. God grant that over the sacrifices that this world crisis will cost an inscription may stand at last like that at Boulder Dam: "For those who died that the desert might bloom."

Spiritual Foundations for a Better World

LISTEN in on almost any conversation about the world's rebuilding after the war, and it is political arrangements that are being discussed. There our thought centers—on one kind of world organization or another, on such questions as national sovereignty, an international police force, tariffs and world-wide economic controls. That such problems are critically important and their solution indispensable, is obvious. But many forget that such international political arrangements are superstructures; they must be built on something in the minds and hearts of the people—on ethical, intellectual, spiritual foundations adequate to sustain them.

What, for example, made the Constitution of the United States a success? The average American now would answer, as a British Prime Minister once said, that the Constitution is "the most wonderful work struck off at a given time by the brain and purpose of man." Yes, but that was said nearly a century afterward. The contemporary fact was that the Constitution was a compromise, fought over with all the bitter difference of opinion that will be involved in any post-war settlement of ours; and in the end it seemed even to the men who framed it so unsatisfactory that of the fifty-five of them, sixteen in disgust refused to sign it, and none of the other thirty-nine was content. What made the Constitution a success was: first, that it was a great document; but second, that underneath it, in the citizens of the colonies, there was enough ethical and spiritual basis and groundwork, enough intelligence, conscience, and loyalty to sustain it and give it a chance. Without that, even the Constitution, as many of its framers fully expected, would have crashed.

"If the foundations be destroyed," cried the writer of the eleventh Psalm, "What can the righteous do?" That verse conjures up a picture full of contemporary meaning: righteous people trying to build an international governmental super-structure, putting into it their best wisdom and labor, only to discover at last that in the minds and hearts of the people there is lacking an intellectual, ethical, spiritual basis adequate to uphold it.

The immediate impact of this emphasis falls on us in the churches. Everyone today criticizes politicians and doubtless they deserve it. But put yourself into the place of these men who at their best are honestly trying to find a way through this jungle to a stable and decent management of the world's affairs. They confront two problems: first, the immensely difficult task of building well the political organization the world needs; but second, that deeper, haunting question—how far will the people follow them, back them up, make the necessary sacrifices that an ordered and peaceful world requires? Are there ethical and spiritual foundations in the people adequate to sustain the kind of world organization we ought to have? That question is religious and ethical, not political; an affair for which not statecraft but homes, schools, churches, and multitudes of individuals, are responsible.

We Christians have been here nearly two thousand years; 650,000,000 professing Christians are in the world today; and still the question rises whether there are spiritual foundations available to sustain a decent organization of mankind's life. We Christians are in no position to blame the statesmen only; we live in a glass house; by this time there ought to be in the hearts of the world's people spiritual bases on which could rest securely a decent world order, and it was our business to build them there. Take the beam out of thine own eye, Christ says to the church, and then thou shalt see clearly to take the mote out of thy brother's, the statesman's, eye. So today I am talking not to statesmen but to the Christian church:

> If the foundations be destroyed,
> What can the righteous do?

Prime Minister Churchill recently said that the League of Nations could have worked successfully. It was organizationally faulty—to be sure it was; but it could have worked. In it there was the possibility of a progressive world order that would have insured peace—if: if the intelligence and conscience of the world had really backed up its intent; if the spiritual quality had been in the world's people to demand of it what was inherent in it, call out from it its effective operation, and pay the price of its endeavor after peace. The League collapsed, not because its political structure, faulty though it was, was hopelessly wrong, but because the ethical and spiritual foundations underneath it were not adequate.

Is that kind of thing going to happen again? For once more that aspect of mankind's problem is paramount, and we may well consider its meaning for us Christians.

For one thing, a decent world order cannot possibly be built upon a basis of pride and self-complacency. Unless all the nations can be brought to the point of penitence, where, humbly conscious of common guilt, they seek common amendment, there is no hope.

One of the worst effects of war is that by its very nature, in every nation engaged in it, it destroys these foundations of humility and penitence. If we are to wage war with the consent of all our faculties we must start with the conviction that we are right, and our enemies wrong; and the longer the war lasts, the more we naturally exalt our own virtues and damn our foes' iniquities. Concerning the relative truth of that none of us would disagree. Hitler is the incarnation of everything I fear and despise most, in national and international life. The Christian church's message involves no soft mitigation of judgment on so appalling an exhibition of antichrist. But the distinctive message of the Christian church does insist on the realistic fact that all of us nations together helped to make Hitler possible; that by what we did not do and by what we did we helped produce him and the opportunity he used; that naziism is the horrid boil in which the base infections of the world have come to a head, and that if the world is to be really cured of its evil, all of us, acknowledging a common guilt, must by God's grace seek amendment together.

I shall say nothing about Russia with its dictatorship, or about Great Britain with its vast problems of imperialism, but surely we in this country ought to see our need of self-searching. Mussolini himself said once about our growing centralization of power in the state that we were one of the Fascist nations; and as for race prejudice, when President Roosevelt says, "There never has been, is not now, and never will be any race of people fit to serve as masters over their fellow men," that strikes home as well as abroad.

The business of the government today is to conquer Hitler; the business of the Christian church is to help conquer hitlerism; and while these two aims have close relationship, they involve different levels of thought and effort. Alas, we can conquer Hitler and still leave hitlerism triumphant! For hitlerism is a philosophy—nationalism so extreme that one's country displaces God; racial prejudice so arrogant that the theory of the master race dominates all life; dictatorship exalted until the state regiments everything and controls everybody; imperialism made into a gospel, as though the mastery and exploitation of subject peoples were the highroad to the new world order; and at the heart of all this, pride—racial and national pride—with not a touch of humility and penitence in it. If that is hitlerism, then obviously hitlerism, far from being Hitler's sin alone, is an evil that tempts every powerful nation, the common guilt and danger, in one degree or another, of all of us, an ethical and spiritual problem that can be solved only by ethical and spiritual means. You cannot kill a philosophy with a gun; you must destroy a philosophy with a philosophy—an ethical evil with an ethical right.

So today the need is urgent, not alone for a new world organization, but for a new spirit on which to build it, and that new spirit can start at only one point—with humility and penitence about ourselves.

The Great Wall of China was a gigantic structure, costing immense expenditure and labor, and when finished it seemed a superb way to gain security; but within a few years of its building it was breached three times by the enemy. Only note: it was breached, not by breaking down the wall, but by bribing the gatekeepers. It was the human element that failed; what collapsed was character, proving insufficient to make the great structure men had reared really work. A like fate awaits us if, absorbed in political tasks, we forget the spiritual foundations.

Let the church, then, lift its voice on behalf of its distinctive message. Once more Christ would say to us what he said in Galilee: "Repent: for the kingdom of heaven is at hand." Says the Old Testament: "All we like sheep have gone astray." Says the New Testament: "There is no distinction; for all have sinned, and fall short of the glory of God." Seen thus from the standpoint of the Eternal, we are all involved in guilt. That message is not emphasized in the public forum, but we ought to hear it in the church; for without such intelligent, objective humility about ourselves, the foundations will not be there on which to build a world organization that can endure.

Consider further that a decent co-operative world order cannot possibly be built upon the basis of vindictiveness and ill will. That statement may seem a platitude, but its significance runs deep. Facing what is likely to happen in our post-war world, two anxieties may well concern us: first, the fear that we may not build wisely that indispensable super-structure of political organization the world needs; but second, the fear that even if in that we should succeed, we yet may fail, not because the superstructure is inadequate but because in the great mass of the world's people the foundations of goodwill—intelligent, farseeing goodwill, that knows the welfare of each to be dependent on the welfare of all—are not there to build on.

A little child, so Dr. Van Kirk tells us, standing on a street curb, saw a small rain puddle with a smear of oil making iridescent colors on it. And the child cried: "Oh, mother, there's a rainbow gone to smash." After the last war a rainbow did go to smash, and if we think the reason is simply a failure in political arrangements, we fool ourselves. Professor Shotwell of Columbia is right when he says: "Our problem is largely an ethical one; it involves recognition on the part of all peoples, large and small, strong and weak, of the rights of others; a willingness on the part of all to make sacrifices for the general good; a belief in the existence of a power in the world that makes for righteousness."

Here again we run upon one of war's worst tragedies. Men, at infinite cost of sacrifice, fight wars for ideal aims—to end war, to win the four freedoms, to establish a co-operative world order; but all the time the processes of war itself undermine the moral foundations of goodwill and mutual understanding on which that better world must rest. So, war after war, another rainbow goes to smash. Let the Christian churches now stand against that swamping of intelligent goodwill by vindictiveness and hatred, for the hope of the world depends on how much farsighted, hardheaded, world-envisioning magnanimity is still here when this war is over.

In this regard I am not half so much concerned about the fighting men at the front as I am about the civilians at home. At the front in the last war, like many of you, I found the vindictiveness and hatred nothing as compared with what they were at home, and in this war the same phenomenon repeats itself. So one of our boys recently wrote to his family: "Maybe this will reassure you—we don't look for a fight but fight like hell when forced into it, and then try to do everything we can to alleviate the suffering we've caused." There is a man with a head on him, maintaining even amid the brutalities of war the kind of spirit on which any decent human life after the war must be built. At the front one commonly finds that spirit—sometimes amazingly finds it, even with reference to the enemy. It is at home that hatred and vindictiveness too often run wild. Was it not Chesterton who once exclaimed: "Hell hath no fury like a non-combatant"?

Our world-problem is political but it is more than that. During the last war C. E. Montague, a brilliant British journalist, went into battle with an intoxicated certainty that the war was all it was idealized to be—a war to end war and make the world safe for democracy. But in 1922, when it was all over and the aftermath was evident, he wrote a book called *Disenchantment*. Why was Montague disenchanted? In 1922 there still were grandiose plans to save the world, vast architectural schemes to organize mankind for peace. But Montague had eyes. He was looking at people, the kind of people who were the building material out of which those architectural marvels must be made, and he wrote: "Just when there seems to be such a babble as never before about these grandiose structures, bricks have run short." That's a haunting phrase! Vast architectural schemes to save the world, but what if bricks run short, the individual ethical stuff out of which all social structures must be made?

In these days a preacher does wish that he could really preach. This business of believing in Christ is so tremendously important now. He is right: vindictive ill will solves no problems; only goodwill in the end builds anything; not softness, not sentimentality, not appeasement—Christ never meant that —but goodwill that marshals intelligence, creates instruments, overrides enmity, outwears ingratitude, and holds in its care the welfare of all mankind with a tenacious magnanimity that

[48]

will not let go. An actor, describing the difference between actors and preachers, said: "We actors talk about imaginary things as though they were real; you preachers talk about real things as though they were imaginary." God forgive us if we do, for those qualities of spirit that Christ incarnated and pleaded for are the real things now on which the hope of the world depends.

> If the foundations be destroyed,
> What can the righteous do?

If the better world we want must be built on humility and penitence, on intelligent goodwill and magnanimity, it certainly must be built on faith and courage. Skepticism and cynicism will not sustain it. We naturally center our attention today on the political conditions of peace, but when a man like Professor MacIver of Columbia University writes a book about the matter,* although politics lies within his specialty, he stresses what he calls the psychological conditions of peace. These are certainly in part the church's business, and how immeasurably important they are! They are the basis of the whole affair.

Some men and women must be here today, tempted, in these terrific times, to give up their Christian faith, to think there is no God, and Christ's way of life a fantastic dream. Before you take that step, I ask you, Do you really believe that the world order we desire—co-operative, implementing human brotherhood, serving the peace and progress of all mankind—can rest upon the basis of such negation? When our founding fathers were framing the Constitution, Benjamin Franklin, eighty-one years old, rose in the convention and said: "I have lived, Sir, a long time; and the longer I live, the more convincing proofs I see of this truth, *that GOD governs in the affairs of men.* And, if a sparrow cannot fall to the ground without his notice, is it probable that an empire

* *Towards an Abiding Peace.*

[49]

can rise without his aid? We have been assured, Sir, in the Sacred Writings, that 'except the Lord build the house, they labor in vain that build it.' I firmly believe this; and I also believe, that, without his concurring aid, we shall succeed in this political building no better than the builders of Babel." Well, do we really think that any great political superstructure can endure without such underpinning?

Let those who surrender Christian ideas and ideals today take cognizance of the company they are joining! Recall the reasons that General Ludendorf after the last war gave for rejecting Christianity. "I reject Christianity," said Ludendorf, "because it is Jewish, because it is international, and because, in cowardly fashion, it preaches peace on earth." So! Those are the reasons because of which Ludendorf, and now the Nazis, who are his successors, reject Christianity. For those three reasons I accept it. It is Jewish, thank God, rooted in the great Hebrew prophets of righteousness, the noblest succession of ethical teachers in the ancient world; it is international, believing in one God and one human family; it does preach peace on earth, knowing that the continuance of war means humanity's suicide. In these days God help us all to take our stand, not with the Ludendorfs, but with the Franklins and Washingtons—not orthodox, not regimented creedalists—free souls, all of them, but deeply grounded in those strong faiths in God and his Eternal Purpose on which alone great structures can be reared. So Dr. Kirtley Mather, Professor of Geology at Harvard, who would never be thought of as a conventional believer, was asked, after an address on his hopes of a better world, what part his faith in God played; and he answered with a clear affirmation of belief ending with this sentence: "Therefore I, too, would couple the brotherhood of man with the fatherhood of God."

Man, tempted to give up your Christian faith, picture, I beg of you, any political superstructure you can imagine, reared on antichrist, as we see antichrist exhibited today, and can you avoid foreseeing its ultimate epitaph: "A foolish man, who built his house upon the sand: and the rain descended, and the floods came, and the winds blew, and smote upon that house; and it fell: and great was the fall thereof"?

Surely this matter of spiritual foundations for a better world is every man's affair. Each one of us either helps or hinders. Most of us can do mighty little directly about the vast political superstructure, but in laying the foundations each of us will have a hand. And

> If the foundations be destroyed,
> What can the righteous do?

Getting the Best Out of the Worst

THE eighty-fourth Psalm describes a kind of person that all of us in these days need to be: "Passing through the valley of Weeping they make it a place of springs." When a man who trusts God, says the psalmist, and has a real experience of Divine resource, finds himself in a forbidding and ominous place—the valley of Weeping, or, as Dr. Moffatt translates it, "Wearyglen"—he can do more than merely get through it; he can creatively make of it something worth while, a place of springs.

To anyone knowing Palestine at firsthand that last phrase has emphatic meaning. All life in Palestine centers around springs. Few and far between, they are still, despite modern waterworks, the indispensable prerequisites of life, so that when the psalmist said that a man passing through disaster makes it a place of springs, he put the matter as strongly as he could. There are souls, he said, who by God's grace know how to win the very best out of the worst.

That this ability is our need now—alike in the armed forces and in the civilian population—everyone must see. Many are cracking up emotionally, nervously, morally, and are coming out of this experience the worse for it, while others are learning lessons they never learned before, having strength called out in them never called out before, and are so handling this experience that they will be wiser and better persons because of it. Which group are we going to belong to? In ordinary life it is clear to anyone who closely watches people that not so much what happens to a man, as the way he takes it and what he does with it, makes the man. But now that fact is accentuated in a vast, world-wide catastrophe, which none can escape, with the question confronting each of us: What are you making of it?

In every decent person one should be able to count on this much to start with: a desire at least not to be among those who merely drag through this crisis or who go to pieces under its stress, but rather among those who creatively make something of it and of themselves in it, and come out of it the wiser and stronger because of it. Week after week the lists of war casualties are published and we read them with bated breath, looking for the names of our friends. But the real list of war casualties is longer than that—unheralded, unpublished, unknown—the men and women who in secret are shot to pieces, their faith wrecked, their morale broken, their ethical principles undone, their emotional life swamped by discouragement and cynicism or by vindictiveness and hate, so that this tremendous experience means to them progressive personal deterioration. They, too, are war casualties. Surely, whatever other obligations this crisis imposes, one central obligation confronts each of us: not to be thus oneself a casualty of war.

Studdert Kennedy was one of the outstanding British chaplains of the last war, and we who were stimulated by his extraordinary personality recall his description of the Last Judgment as he conceived it. When he stood before the eternal judgment seat, he said, he expected God to ask him just one question: Well, what did you make of it?

This morning we concern ourselves with that question and with the inquiry it suggests: What causes some people to come out worse, and some to come out better from such an experience as this? What are the qualities of mind and character that enable a man passing through this valley of Weeping to make it a place of springs?

For one thing, some people in a disastrous era like this take the attitude merely of endurance, of somehow or other managing to stand it, while others are all waked up by it, intellectually and spiritually stimulated, so that they learn things they never saw before.

How natural that negative attitude of mere endurance is now, everybody knows. I would not disparage it; it is an essential part of the picture; the quality of endurance can be a noble virtue. By itself alone, however, merely to say of one of the most stupendous crises in all history: I will manage somehow stoically to live it through, is not enough; and as the months and years wear on it easily turns into dull, stolid, and then weary, self-pitying. In times like this such a mood is natural, but let a man live on it long enough and he is bound to be a war casualty. Our admiration instinctively goes out to another kind of person—intellectually and spiritually waked up by this crisis to see things he never saw before, learn things he never learned before, and become something he never was before.

If someone says that this difference between people is temperamental and not altogether within our control, I grant that. In Italy the Congressional Medal of Honor was recently given to a soldier who in the thick of battle, when everything was going wrong, suddenly took matters into his own hands, waged what the communiqués call a "one man war," performing incredible exploits; and when he was asked how on earth he ever came to do that he answered simply, "I just got mad." To be sure, that kind of response to a desperate situation—not merely enduring it but being all waked up by it—is in part temperamental, but it is not all temperamental. We ordinary folk can have something to say as to whether we join the company of the dour, who merely manage to get by, or the company of those who are intellectually and spiritually aroused to think and do and be what was never within their scope before. The papers recently told us of a woman, chased by her angry husband, who jumped clean over a seven foot fence. I am not asking that of you, but even that says something to us: an evil situation can be one of the most stimulating experiences one ever meets.

To be sure, these are depressing times. Total war, armed with modern weapons, has turned out to be the most ghastly experience in history. Nevertheless, a man has no business merely to endure it; some of the most important lessons humanity ever learned were learned in tragic times. When we think of the world as a whole, we see this. If humanity as a whole, we say, can learn nothing from this experience that will arouse mankind to build something new, then humanity is well-nigh hopeless. But everything the world as a whole learns, is learned first of all by persons like ourselves, one by one, aroused by an evil time to think as we never thought before and be what we never were before—by men and women, that is, who, passing through the valley of Weeping, make it a place of springs.

Deeper yet, however, runs the difference between those who are made worse and those who are made better by a time like this. Some are emotionally infected by the passions of wartime, swamped by its bitterness, its prejudice, its hatred and vengefulness; while others are enlarged in their vision to take the whole world in, to feel as they never felt before its unity and interdependence, to see the impossibility of welfare for any without the welfare of all—and so are made not less but more citizens of the world and patriots for humanity. Immensely important that difference is! The question confronts each of us today: Are we coming out of this experience the more bitter-spirited, prejudiced and vindictive, or the more humane, world-envisioning and magnanimous?

In ordinary life we continually reveal our own quality by what we see in things and get out of them. Here are two men, for example, reading the Bible—Whittier and Whistler—Whittier, the good gray Quaker poet; and Whistler, the artist. What did they get out of the Bible? They both tell us. Says Whittier:

The starry pages promise-lit
With Christ's Evangel over-writ.

But Whistler did not get that out of the Bible, for while Whistler had admirable qualities, he was at heart a stormy and bitter controversialist, so that few things in the English language are more harsh and ill tempered than his verbal attacks upon his critics and even his former friends. What, then, did Whistler get out of the Bible? "That splendid mine of invective"—so he once described it.

If even the Bible to a bitter-spirited man can be a mine of invective, what can a wartime era like this be? Here is one of the major tragedies of war, that out of it men get hatred, vengefulness, national and racial prejudice, and then these things that war produces in turn produce war again—and so the vicious cycle goes endlessly on. Thus in nature, failure of rain produces a desert, and then because it is a desert there can be no condensation of moisture, and so, no rain; and in consequence, Sahara, going on century after century, failure of rain making a desert, and a desert causing failure of rain. God save us after this war from such a vicious cycle!

If, however, we are to be saved from it, the cure must begin now in folk like us. In these fearful days one's admiration turns to some souls in history who in desperate times made a creative response that ushered in a new era—to the great Isaiah of the Exile, for example. Listen as Isaiah hears God saying to him: "It is too light a thing that thou shouldest be my servant to raise up the tribes of Jacob, and to restore the preserved of Israel: I will also give thee for a light to the Gentiles, that thou mayest be my salvation unto the end of the earth." So! Centuries before Christ a great soul rose to a world-wide vision that took in all humanity and caught sight of a horizon mankind has never been able to forget, and the miracle is that the man who saw that vision was in the worst valley of Weeping his people ever faced—the Babylonian Exile. It was sheer disaster, full of bitterness, hatred, and violence, yet see what he made of it! Ah, Isaiah, we Christians need to catch your spirit now. You translated an embittered time not into more bitterness but into a world-envisioning hope and devotion that took in all humanity. You did what we all want mankind as a whole to do now, but what we find it desperately difficult to do, one by one, ourselves; passing through the valley of Weeping, you made it a place of springs.

Deeper yet, however, runs this difference between those who come out of this crisis worse, and those who come out better. Some face exhausted spiritual resources, so that their inner strength and courage peter out, while others, needing deeper levels of power to carry on, tap them, and thus grow in adequacy—the greater strain bringing out the greater strength.

Even in ordinary life this difference constitutes one of the most crucial contrasts between persons. Starting, as we all do, with familiar and comparatively easy demands, we run soon or late into some situation—difficult, tragic, perilous—that asks of us more power than life ever asked of us before, and so forces on us the question: Have we no more available resources than our familiar days have called for, or are there deeper levels of power to be drawn on, so that whatever life faces us with, by God's grace we can match it, the need calling out the power? In these days that demand becomes critical. The men in the armed forces are certainly facing it.

Here lies the basic reason why difficulty, danger, tragedy, crisis, wreck some people, but in others call out character that the world never can forget. Watch Abraham Lincoln grow from stature to stature, as burdens become heavier and tragedy deeper, revealing qualities that no one who knew him in his youth would have dreamed were there, and one sees strain bringing out strength, need calling out power, so that passing through his valley of Weeping he did make it a place of springs.

If a man's religious faith does not mean this to him, something deeply is the matter with it. Our message this morning involves a gospel as old as the psalmist, and as new as some youth here who in need of adequate spiritual power to carry on has found it available for his daily use. A child beside the ocean on a rainy day, seeing the water in the bay rise ever higher, cries that the rain is filling up the sea. But a mature man knows that no rain could do that; it is the tide coming in from the great deep. So, too, a man grown mature in mind and spirit knows that all the raining he can do will not fill up his empty bay; that only when the tide, called to by the skies, comes in from deeps beyond his making, can his need be met.

That experience of available spiritual power from beyond ourselves is central in all great religion. Across the centuries churches have risen and fallen, theologies come and gone; but at the heart of great religion, by whatever name it has been called, this experience has gone on: persons strengthened with might by God's spirit in the inner man, an experience too real to be doubted, too universal to be denied. Life need not defeat us; we need not crack up. Even in a time like this we need not merely be resigned to bear our troubles; we can creatively do something with it, make something of it and of ourselves in the midst of it.

In a recent cartoon a clerk in a bookstore, anxious to be helpful, says to a customer, "I am very sorry, we are all out of Bibles, but we have something just as good." I doubt that! Whatever else it is, the Bible is a great book of biography— real men and women who, facing all the hells that evil circumstance and man's iniquity can make on earth, found available for daily use inward power, so that across the centuries they wrought out the most amazing ethical and spiritual development in mankind's record—out of one valley of Weeping after another making a place of springs—until Christ found his

"Wearyglen" at Gethsemane and Calvary, and made of it a place of springs, indeed.

There are two ways in which we can take a situation like this. We can take it as an alibi, an excuse; and if one starts on that course there is no limit to what one can allow oneself to be and do. A chaotic, diabolical era like this can excuse anything in character and conduct if a man wants to use it so, and alas, many do. But this situation, like all trouble and difficulty, can be taken not as an alibi but as raw material out of which something must, and can, be made. A whole philosophy is wrapped up in that simple statement. Watching people, one sometimes thinks that most of them expect to find life ready-made, and hope to find it fortunate and happy. But we never find life; all we find is raw material, sometimes rough stuff and at first sight unpromising, but still, raw material out of which we have to make life. Existence is what we find; life is what we make, and in these days *that* requires the deep, interior resources of spiritual power that spring from inward fellowship with God.

Traveling to Washington on the Pennsylvania Railroad, have you noticed the sign displayed at the town of Chester: "What Chester makes, makes Chester"? A good motto, that! It is not what a man finds in life that matters most—he may find a valley of Weeping—it is what he makes of it that counts. Always, "What Chester makes, makes Chester."

This, then, is the conclusion of the matter: if, in such ways as we have named, we are creatively to turn our valley of Weeping into a place of springs—not merely enduring it but stimulated by it and learning from it, not embittered but enlarged and made more world-conscious because of it, not crushed but discovering new depths of Divine resource in meeting it—we must keep our faith, and not let this evil time shatter that. People commonly talk as though they could believe in God only in fair weather. Tragedy, catastrophe, bereavement lead them to doubt God. But the God of this universe is too great to be completely revealed in fair weather only. We who love the sea have seen it on summer days when its unruffled waters lay quiet and breezeless in the sun. But we have seen it, too, when storm clouds rolled up black and menacing, and the waves were tumultuous with wind, and the angry water shone lurid in the flashes of the lightning. It takes stormy as well as sunny days to reveal all the meaning of the sea. So God is love, but he is judgment, too; and today the God of judgment is revealed. It is terrific, but in just such times as these great souls have seen deepest into God's meaning and his will, have learned most, grown strongest, and made some of the most notable advances in history.

Studdert Kennedy was right. Every one of us will face the judgment seat, with one question asked of him: What did you make of it?

The Common Sense Wisdom of Christianity

THESE are difficult days for idealists. To call a man perfectionist and idealistic is to condemn him as unfit for a time when realism and hardheadedness are plainly called for; and because, of all ways of living, the Christian ethic is thought of as most idealistic, these are hard days for Christianity. The characteristic ideas of Christian goodness, men say, are irrelevant to this violent scene, the Sermon on the Mount obviously out of gear with our cruel necessities of action and impossibly perfectionist in this tough world.

A friend of mine once saw Mont Blanc, its snow-capped summit glorious in the sun, while its base was hidden in the clouds, so that the glistening crest, snow-white and sun drenched, seemed to float high in the air, unattached to the solid earth. Resplendent it was, but like a fairyland—impossible of access and unbased on anything solid and factual. So to many appears the Christian way of life—ideal indeed, they say, but impossibly ideal in such a world.

This way of looking at the matter, natural though it is, neglects a persistent emphasis of the Bible in general and of Jesus in particular. Ask what the great prophets and the Master were most concerned to create in men, and the ordinary answer would be "goodness." Ideal righteousness, justice, and love, we say, are the qualities the Scripture seeks. True enough! But why leave out that other central matter—wisdom? No such word as "ideal" can be found in the Bible, but one great passage after another calls for wisdom against folly. That the Master wanted men to be good is obvious, but he appealed also to men to be wise—"wise as serpents," he said, as well as "harmless as doves." He likened his generation, facing the gospel, to ten maidens, five of whom were wise, and five foolish; and seeing men so good that they could be called "children of light" he nonetheless condemned them because they were not so wise as "the children of this world." Such was the nature of the Master's message, and when he brought his Sermon on the Mount to its resounding conclusion, he said, as Dr. Moffatt translates it, "Everyone who listens to these words of mine and acts upon them will be like a sensible man, who built his house on rock."

If the Christian way of life is thus wisdom, we need to understand that fact, for the present collapse of civilization is a colossal advertisement of man's folly. What if, in thinking of the Christian life as perfectionist, we miss the point, and what if for men and nations Christ is what Paul called him: "The wisdom of God"?

This shift of emphasis from ideal goodness to wisdom is pertinent even in ordinary times. Here is a youth facing some critical decision, with an older person—his father or mother or counselor—anxiously watching his strong and dangerous drift toward a mistaken choice. To be sure, it is a choice between right and wrong, goodness and sin, the ideal and the unideal, but with what urgency, when the last ditch is reached, does that other appeal surge up: Don't make a fool of yourself! Until we hear Jesus saying that, we have not understood him. To us today as men and nations, that, most of all, he seems to be saying: Stop making fools of yourselves! "Everyone who listens to these words of mine and does not act upon them," so Dr. Moffatt translates the familiar verse, "will be like a stupid man, who built his house on sand."

As we try to understand this approach to the Christian way of life, consider first that we run into something like it whenever we deal seriously with the problem of knowledge. The pride of our modern world has been our knowledge, which we have trusted to make us wise. Such vast accessions of new information in so brief a time mankind never experienced before, but today the world's catastrophe makes it evident that

...e and wisdom are not identical. About one matter
...s everlastingly right: something ethical and spiritual
... added to knowledge before it becomes wisdom. As
... said: "Knowledge comes, but wisdom lingers."
... unken father driving his motor car wrecked it and
... is two-year-old son, seriously injuring a friend and
... his children. That man had knowledge our fathers
... dreamed, and controlled power a few years ago un-
... able. But alas, all that did not make him wise! We may
not, therefore, push aside the idea that Christ's way of life
is wisdom on the ground that knowledge alone is adequate.
Recently a pathetic letter came from a man messing up his
life with such emotional and moral disorder as threatens
everything he cares for most, and at the letter's end was this
exclamation: "It just beats me! A Ph.D., and unable to
solve my own troubles."

This emphasis upon the fact that knowledge and wisdom
are not the same thing involves no lack of appreciation of
the benefits our new knowledge has conferred. They are immense. To all pioneers of research and education, to the ex-
plorers of our new science and the builders of our great
schools, we are unpayably indebted. Yet look at the world
today! It takes more than knowledge to make us wise.
Thoreau meant this when, hearing a friend boast of the mani-
fold branches of knowledge taught at Harvard College, he exclaimed, "Yes, indeed, all the branches and none of the roots."
That was hard on Harvard and doubtless undeserved; but
still one of our college graduates said recently: "College gave
us spokes but no hub. We came away with knowledge but no
purpose, and therein is our dilemma."

How much deeper a thing wisdom is than intellect alone!
Wisdom involves spiritual insight, integrity of character, an
understanding love of things worth loving, a scale of values
that puts first things first, and transcendent loyalties to which
one's soul is given, all unified by a philosophy of life that

[63]

puts worth-while meaning and purpose into living. Only such attributes of the spirit ever yet made any man wise. When, therefore, Christ pleads with us for these very things, and we call him "perfectionist," and "idealistic," we miss the point. Rather, today, in a world that desperately needs it, he calls for wisdom. Science alone cannot save us, but instead furnishes us with the very instruments for our self-destruction, because science alone cannot make us wise. Education alone cannot save us, though we reduce illiteracy to the point of vanishing, because the education of the intellect alone never yet made men wise. To be wise involves, along with what the mind knows, what the spirit is, the values the soul loves, and the faiths by which it is persuaded. So, as the Scripture cries,

> Wisdom is the principal thing; therefore get wisdom;
> Yea, with all thy getting get understanding.

We confront this same truth when we deal not only with knowledge but with personal morals. The finest ethical traditions of our race come from the accumulated wisdom of mankind. In these chaotic days we are morally disordered, and the dreadful words of Thucydides about war, spoken centuries ago, prove true still: "War is a savage teacher which brings men's characters down to the level of their fortunes." Nevertheless, we do have some high ethical traditions about what great character really is and what great living means, and these best traditions come from the accumulated wisdom of the race.

In these days of separated families, for example, we naturally recall our great traditions about the kind of family life most worth having. Some of us have had homes where these traditions were fulfilled, and now as life comes toward its evening the choicest memories of our years are associated with them, and our dearest hope for our children and grandchildren is that they may have homes like that. Shall we, then, call these best traditions of family life idealistic? That will not do. These noblest ideas of the home have sprung from the accumulated wisdom of the race—watching family life for centuries, seeing what happens in homes, trying every conceivable experiment, and saying at last, This is wisdom; this is the kind of home most worth having. No one understands our best ethical traditions until he stops interpreting them as perfectionist idealism and begins seeing them as the race's accumulated wisdom.

If someone here is tempted to think of a home where two people love each other as they love no one else at all, and throw around their growing children the abiding security of a loyal family, as a perfectionist ideal, let him listen to a tough-minded man, Mr. J. Edgar Hoover, of the Federal Bureau of Investigation, realistically concerned about the nation and its future: "Too many homes in America are broken. Divorce, crime and bad example have made irreparable inroads. There is a clear indication of adult failure to impress on the minds of youth, those principles of faith, morality and personal conduct which have stood the test of centuries." So! The high tradition of the family at its best is not perfectionist idealism but social wisdom and social necessity. It says to us, as though with the very words of Jesus: Every one therefore that heareth these words of mine, and doeth them, shall be likened unto a wise man, who built his home upon the rock.

Or shift the field of illustration to those more intimate affairs of personal character where modern psychology can speak. No confirmation of Jesus' basic ethic is more impressive today than that which comes from the best of the psychiatrists. You must lose life to find it, said Jesus—expend it to have it, give it to keep it. That, says the common man, is a perfectionist ideal. But with one voice the great psychiatrists say, No! That is wisdom; no self-centered life is a healthy life.

> I gave a little tea party
> This afternoon at three.
> 'Twas very small, three guests in all
> I, myself and me.

Myself ate up the sandwiches
While I drank all the tea
'Twas also I who ate the pie
And passed the cake to me.

To escape from *that*, which is the very essence of damnation, into a life that has found its loyalty, belongs to something, and has gained life by losing it, is no perfectionist idealism but wisdom.

Do not hate, says Jesus, not even your enemies. That, says the common man, is perfectionism. But with one voice the great psychologists say, No! Hate is about the most disintegrating force that can disrupt a human life, and whatever it does to anybody else, it obscures the intelligence, deranges the judgment, roils the emotions, and embitters the life of the one who cherishes it.

In one realm after another in these days the emphasis thus shifts, in the interpretation of Jesus' teaching, from idealism to wisdom. One grows tired of hearing the Sermon on the Mount described as perfectionism. Do we really like the people who today agree with that opinion? Anyone tempted to hold that Jesus' teaching on the Mount is wild idealism may well consider this quotation from a Nazi book used now in Nazi schools, entitled, *Judenfibel*, "Jew Primer": "The teaching of mercy and love of one's neighbor is foreign to the German race and the Sermon on the Mount is, according to Nordic sentiment, an ethic for cowards and idiots." That is a slander on the German race; we know too many splendid German Christians to believe that about their race; but it is true about the Nazis, and it should give point to what we are saying here. How do we like the consequence of thinking, really, that the Sermon on the Mount is idiotic idealism? Thinking that puts us into a kind of company we should not be pleased to join. This war against naziism will not be fully won until that idea is overthrown and once more the Sermon on the Mount is seen to be wisdom.

Indeed, when some unchristian conduct of ours has run its course and in personal disgrace or social shame, humiliated with the sense of guilt and the fact of failure, we repent, what form does our penitence naturally take? For myself, I do not think first how bad I have been but what a fool I have been. Repeatedly across the years, our personal penitence has confirmed what we are saying here: What ought to have been done was wise—as Cowper said, "Wisdom and Goodness are twin born"—and now, caught in the aftermath of our misdeeds, we cry, God be merciful to me a fool!

We confront this same truth not only when we deal with knowledge and personal morals but with our social hopes. Long ago a Hebrew prophet said that the time would come when men would "beat their swords into plowshares, and their spears into pruning-hooks," and learn war no more. For centuries men have called that an impossible ideal and have scoffed at such perfectionism. Not only did Nietzsche say, "It is the good war which halloweth every cause," but Renan, the Frenchman, said, "War is one of the conditions of progress, the cut of the whip which prevents a country from going to sleep," and Ruskin, the Englishman, said, "War is the foundation of all the arts, . . . of all the high virtues and faculties of men," and Lester Ward, the American sociologist, said, "War has been the chief and leading condition of human progress." So the tough-minded have espoused war and developed it until now the world confronts total war, in the face of which even the hardest heads begin to change their tune.

For total war means four things. First, no great nation can stay out of it; it is global; all people are involved. Second, no individual can escape it; it penetrates every home and works its most appalling consequences not so much on warriors as on civilians, not alone on armies but on women and children. Third, no area of life is free from its regimented

[67]

domain; it sweeps everything—our science, our economics, our politics, our personal liberties—under its dictatorial control. Fourth, it is permanent, not stopping when the fighting stops but persisting in economic conflict, racial antagonism, and nationalistic anarchy that insanely treat this now condensed and unified world as though it were the old world of isolated communities and unconquered distances.

Today, therefore, even the toughest minds begin to see that a world organized for peace is no perfectionist ideal but social wisdom and social necessity. How many more world wars will it take before the last vestige of our personal liberty is gone and our democracy collapses like a house of cards? When today we read in the New Testament that we are "members one of another," that it cannot be well with any until it is well with all, that whatsoever we would that men should do unto us, we had better do unto them, is it not as though a voice long despised were speaking again: Verily I say unto you, a world that hears these words of mine and doeth them, shall be likened unto a wise man, who built his house upon a rock?

Granted, that we must not oversimplify this matter! Granted, that Christianity is too great to be crowded within the boundaries of any single word, even "wisdom"! To face the cross and choose *that* rather than be untrue does break over the confines of common sense, and demands more latitude and longitude than the word "wise" includes. Yet even there, if Christ had to choose again, would he choose differently? Was Judas wise? Was Jesus foolish?

Indeed, when one thinks not alone of Jesus' ethic but of his religious faith and life, is that perfectionist idealism? To have a secret place where one can meet the Eternal Spirit and draw reserves of daily power, to have a sustaining faith undergirding character and supporting sacrificial loyalty, to see what is highest in ourselves backed by what is deepest in the universe, and so to live as Paul said, "stedfast, unmovable,

ays abounding in the work of the Lord" because we know
our "labor is not vain in the Lord"—is not that wise?
n Santayana said,

> It is not wisdom to be only wise,
> And on the inward vision close the eyes.

Behind all other choices today is this choice as to where
real wisdom lies. In 1908 a book was published in France
entitled, *La Folié de Jésus*, "The Insanity of Jesus," in which
the author said that in nineteenth-century Europe Jesus would
have been put under restraint as a megalomaniac afflicted with
mystical hallucinations of a kind well known to clinical medicine. So! This modern world has been wise, and Jesus is
insane? This spectacle now spread before us is common
sense, and he is mad? Well, during the Civil War they told
Lincoln that Grant was a drunkard, and Lincoln answered
that he wished he knew what kind of liquor Grant drank,
that he might get some for his other generals. So one who
cares about mankind might wish today that Jesus' madness
would infect us all, for if to be sane is to be like our modern
world, and if to be mad is to be Christlike, then insanity were
our profoundest need.

When Sir Isaac Newton announced the law of gravitation,
men talked about him just as men still talk about Jesus. Said
one man, Newton has a "deranged poetical fancy." Said
another critic, "This crazy mathematician will not have twenty
followers in his lifetime." Well that was true. Newton lived
forty years after the publication of his book, and his converts
numbered less than a dozen. But at last, one by one, and then
in masses, men faced an astonishing experience as it dawned
on them that Newton's revelation was not deranged poetical
fancy but fact, astounding fact and universal law. Such a
profound change will some day alter mankind's judgment
concerning Jesus.

May that insight come to some youth here, not so much

saying to him, Stop being unideal, as saying, Stop making a fool of yourself! And to all of us, men and nations, may the truth grow clear which the old story of Jesus' birth enshrines in an unforgettable picture: "Now when Jesus was born in Bethlehem of Judaea in the days of Herod the king, behold, Wisemen from the east. . . . And they came into the house and saw the young child . . . and they fell down and worshipped him."

Taking Jesus Seriously

LUKE'S Gospel tells us that after Simon Peter had come to know Jesus, had had Jesus in his own home, had been welcomed by him to discipleship, and had begun to see the kind of person he was and the work he did, he "fell down at Jesus' knees, saying, Depart from me; for I am a sinful man, O Lord."

At first sight that seems a strange response to make to the Master. To become acquainted with the most glorious character that ever came to earth and then to cry, as Dr. Moffatt translates it, "Lord, leave me; I am a sinful man"— what kind of response is that to the beauty and strength of Jesus? But on second thought that is taking Jesus seriously, and without that there is no such thing as taking him seriously. Simon Peter was right—when in any earnest fashion a man sees Christ, if he knows himself at all and with any reality apprehends the transcendent personality of the Master, his first response is not a satisfied admiration, adoration, worship, but a cry from the depths of conscience: Go away from me; you disturb me; I do not belong to your scale of life; I cannot rise to what you ask; leave me, for I am a sinful man, O Lord! That is taking Jesus in earnest.

Anyone acquainted with Christian thought during the last generation knows that at this point we are saying something that needs to be said. Many people have pretty much reduced their Christianity to admiration of Jesus—an admiration taken for granted as easy, natural, and to be expected. Of course, we admire Jesus—almost everyone says that. I have no use for your Christian doctrine, says one; I will have nothing to do with your Christian churches, says another, but of course, I admire Jesus.

[71]

You recall Sidney Lanier's poem in which, reviewing the great characters of history, he finds in every one of them something that needs to be forgiven. But when he thinks of Jesus, he says,

> What *if* or *yet*, what mole, what flaw, what lapse,
> What least defect or shadow of defect,
> What rumor, tattled by an enemy,
> Of inference loose, what lack of grace
> Even in torture's grasp, or sleep's, or death's,—
> Oh, what amiss may I forgive in Thee,
> Jesus, good Paragon, thou Crystal Christ?

Many consent to that. They admire Jesus' character—that is about all the Christianity they have. But in these desperate days I should suppose it evident that that is not enough. Admire Christ? But Christ is no beautiful sunset concerning which it is sufficient to say, How lovely it is! Look at our generation, outdoing the beasts in beastliness, and at our own lives, stained by all the outward evil we deplore, and then look at Christ! Simon Peter was right—he is not simply admirable but terrible. He is the most disturbing personality we ever face. We do not instinctively run to him. Instinctively we try to escape him. Give him his way and it means the upset of our world, and as for our own lives, we cannot live with ourselves and with him at the same time. Anyone who takes Christ in earnest begins where Simon Peter began, "Lord, leave me; I am a sinful man."

Start, for example, with Christ's teaching. It is difficult to find anyone who does not admire it. One of the easiest ways to get applause in America is to praise the Sermon on the Mount. Much of our preaching has consisted in that—how noble Jesus' ethical precepts are; who does not admire them? For myself, however, I could not preach a sermon like that to save my life. To be sure, the Sermon on the Mount is noble. That is the trouble. Reading it, one sometimes feels as a moron might feel reading a university catalogue. Of course, that catalogue is marvelous, offering all this wealth of opportunity, but a moron would want most of all to throw it away and never think of it again. Something drastic and miraculous must happen to him before the transcendent privileges of the university are within his dimension. Well, look at our world and at our lives in comparison with the ethical precepts of the Master: the contrast and disproportion are appalling. A man who has not so felt about the Sermon on the Mount has never taken it seriously.

Or, consider Jesus as a personal example. To be a Christian, we say—and we often say it smoothly and easily—is to make Jesus our ideal and to follow in his steps. Indeed, that very phrase is Simon Peter's. Long afterwards, when he wrote his Epistle, he said that Christ suffered for us, leaving us an example, that we should follow in his steps. But he did not say that at first. A first he saw too clearly the gulf that separated him from Christ to talk about taking him for an example. He felt like a sick man seeing some magnificent Sandow stalk before him, great in stature, perfect in physique —attractive, yes, but maddening too, making his own weakness odious by comparison. What could he in his frailty have to do with an ideal like that? Leave me alone, he cried!

So, in our day, in words that to some easy-going Christians would seem at first intolerably irreverent, Dorothy Sayers has interpreted this initial response to Jesus:

> Thou liest, Christ, Thou liest; take it hence,
> That mirror of strange glories; I am I;
> What wouldst Thou make of me? O cruel pretence,
> Drive me not mad so with the mockery
> Of that most lovely, unattainable lie!

Someone, however, may be saying that to be a Christian is not so much legalistically to obey Christ's teaching, or imitatively to follow in his steps, as it is to catch his spirit. Often we hear Christianity so described. As though we were simplifying matters, we say that to be a Christian is to catch Christ's spirit. But that is the hardest thing of all. Once Jesus took a towel, and, girding himself, washed his disciples' feet. In Palestine that act was so familiar that the disciples had seen it countless times, but when Jesus did it, a solemn hush fell on them, and in that simple deed a quality and meaning were present that they never could forget. What is this inner radiance, this mystic gift of spiritual grace that illumines common deeds until they become immortal, and turns even the ordinary breaking of bread into an undying sacrament? And now men say that we are to catch that spirit of Jesus and so be Christian. My soul, at that point most of all I understand Simon Peter: O Lord, leave me, for I am a sinful man.

See what we are trying to say! When one really sees Jesus and takes him seriously—his teaching, his example, his spirit —the Master can be the most forbidding and shaming figure that ever walked the earth.

What, then, is the way out, for the New Testament makes it plain that there is a way out. The New Testament is the most triumphant book in man's spiritual history. It starts where Simon Peter started, but it does not stop there. All the way through it are men and women made poignantly aware of their sin and shame, yet all the way through it runs the note of spiritual victory, too, and the reason is not simply emotional but intellectual. This situation we have described drove those first Christians to some profound thinking that we modern Christians, who in easy times have grown superficial, in these serious days need to reproduce.

To begin with, those first Christians thought their problem through until they saw that Jesus is more than Jesus; he is the revelation of the Eternal. How profound a difference it makes in any realm when something is seen as more than itself— the revelation of the Eternal! When some great scientist, a genius unapproachable by us, with brilliant insight beyond our power at first even to understand, discovers some world-transforming truth, he could be, thought of only as an individual, utterly shaming and discouraging to us, who, with pedestrian minds can follow him only afar off. But that, thank heaven, is not the whole truth. Galileo, Newton, Watts, and all the rest, are more than individuals. They are revealers of the eternal, opening up new realms of truth and power, which, once opened up, we ordinary folk can enter into and avail ourselves of. So Simon Peter's first revulsion from Christ, impossibly beyond him, turned to hope. Jesus was more than Jesus: he was the revealer of the Eternal Spirit, who could come into our lives, too. "The God of all grace," wrote Peter years afterwards in his Epistle, "who called you unto his eternal glory in Christ . . . shall himself perfect, establish, strengthen you."

When winter gives way to spring, the first sign we see appears in some tree or shrub whose leaves begin to clothe with green the branches that have long been bare. If that tree were merely an individual, how slight its meaning and how disheartening its verdure to other trees still barren! But far from being an individual alone, what we are really seeing in that single tree is a revelation of awakening life, cosmic in its source, universal in its reach, that can come up into all living things and recreate them. That is not discouraging. That is great good news. So to these first Christians Jesus was more than Jesus. He was the Logos, they said, the Word of God, God's expression, the forth-going of the Eternal, revealing himself in one life, that he might make himself available to all.

To be sure, the doctrine of the divinity of Jesus has been grossly mistreated by theology and often put into terms incredible to minds like ours. But it is a pity because of that to miss the tremendous import of its meaning. Jesus' manhood alone, transcendent in quality and unapproachable by us, does call out Simon Peter's first response. But what if Jesus is more than Jesus? What if he reveals the Spirit of the living God, in whom we too live and move and have our being, and who in us can work the miracle of his creative spring-time? That is gospel. Peter started by crying in shame before Jesus' human character, Leave me, for I am a sinful man, but he ended by saying in triumph, "Thou art the Christ, the Son of the living God."

So one young man recently said in my presence, "It takes Jesus' godhead to resurrect us from the despair into which his manhood plunges us." There is truth in that. Tell me that Jesus is only an individual man and that I must be like him, and I quit. At that point I know enough about myself to quit, as in Browning's poem, Andrea del Sarto stands before Raphael's painting and cries,

> But all the play, the insight and the stretch—
> Out of me, out of me!

Tell me, however, that Christ is the revelation of the Eternal Spirit, opening up a realm of Divine life and power into which I too can enter, and that is gospel. Then, humbly but really, when I face Christ, I can say, "Spirit of God, descend upon my heart."

Again, those first Christians thought their problem through until they saw that Jesus is more than Jesus—not simply a teacher and a personal ideal but the pioneer of a new age on earth for all mankind. What a difference that makes!

America's first trained nurse, Linda Richards, died in 1930. Fourteen years ago the first trained nurse in America was still with us. Now, Linda Richards was important as an individual, but no one who stops with that sees her full significance. She was more than an individual; she was a pioneer, a trail-blazer, the harbinger of a new era in the life of all sick folk in America. She was the beginning of some-thing that is to go on and on beyond herself to greater things. How much more is that true of the Master! Tell us only that he is the perfect man standing there in history, and we shall feel as Simon Peter did at first; but tell us that he is the pioneer of a new age that shall in the end change the quality and transform the relationships of all mankind, and that is not discouraging. That is what the New Testament calls it—news, good news.

The Wright brothers are to us more than individuals. They were pioneers, and while what they did we never could have done, now that they have done it every one of us can share in the new era that they opened up. So the New Testament thinks of Jesus—more than a teacher, more than an example, he opened the gates of a new age, changed B.C. to A.D., introduced into history a new force, let loose in the world a new dynamic that can, and does, and will, change human life and transform human relationships. That is what they meant when they called him the Messiah. Logos—that means that he is the revealer of the Eternal Spirit. Messiah—that means that he is the pioneer of a new age. When Simon Peter saw that truth about him he completely changed his tune. Christ, the Messiah of a new humanity—that was the best news he had ever heard.

Tschaikowsky said that he gave himself to music because of Mozart. "It is thanks to Mozart," he wrote, "that I have devoted my life to music." So Mozart was his messiah, the pioneer for him of a new era in music, and whenever he speaks of Mozart one feels two tones in his voice: first, humility before superior excellence, but second, stimulus, challenge, hope. He could not have introduced the new era, he feels, but Mozart could, and now that it is here he can share it and in it play a part. Well, Christ is much more than Mozart and we much less than Tschaikowsky, but still the truth there lights up our relationship with our Lord. If Christ were only a teacher, telling us what we ought to do, if he were only an individual ideal, telling us to be like himself, then we would be discouraged. But he is more than that. He is, as the New Testament calls him, "the pioneer" of our salvation. What he did we never could have done, but now that he has done it we can share in it and play our part in its coming triumph. That is not discouraging. That is a great gospel.

Again, those first disciples thought their problem through until they saw that Jesus is more than Jesus; not simply teacher and example, he is a savior, too. An immense difference that makes!

One wonders what Jesus said to Simon Peter—beyond the single sentence that the Gospel records—when, penitent, he threw himself at the Master's knees and said, "Depart from me; for I am a sinful man." One can imagine Christ speaking to him thus:

> Simon, it is just because you are a sinful man that I have come to you. That is what I am here for. You tell me to leave you because you are sinful. Man, that is why I came—because men are sinful. I understand why you shrink from me. A sick man is not helped when some paragon of physical perfection stands in his presence, an ideal of health to taunt his weakness, but do not take me so! I am the good physician. Your sickness is the reason I have come, not to taunt you but to heal you. Take me thus, not as teacher and example only but as savior.

Throughout the New Testament that gospel runs. If Jesus is only our ideal, then we are of all men most miserable, but if he is our savior, too, then the doors of hope begin to open.

Who does not feel the need of this today? I do not know that I need any more ideals. The ideals I have for myself and for the world are so tantalizingly beyond reach that they are disheartening, and to tell me worshipfully to admire Jesus as the great ideal, does not help the situation. See what we human brutes are doing to one another on the earth today, all of us involved in the causes, processes, and results of man's diabolical iniquity, and for medicine what if no more can be said than that Jesus is our ideal? What we need is a savior. If Christ is that, if transforming powers are by the grace of God released through him that can remake us men and women, here is hop... is not that why he came? Is not ...ending that wi... it means to take him in earnest?

...op Booth, of Vermont, lived all too short a life, but ...it lasted it was profoundly Christian. After he died his ...said to a friend, "I know where the Bishop is tonight. ...ul has gone to hell." The friend was too shocked to speak, but then the nurse went on, "That's the only place he can be happy; there's such work to do there." That was Jesus' spirit. He sought out hell. He hungered for sinful men. Today in this congregation of supposedly elect spirits he is moving still, saying, "They that are whole have no need of a physician, but they that are sick: I came not to call the righteous, but sinners."

Ah, Christ—our teacher, our example, but more than that: revealer of the eternal grace of God, pioneer of a new humanity, our physician and savior! So there is hope!

A Kind of Penitence That Does Some Good

ONE of the most prevalent emotions in the hearts of intelligent and sensitive people today is the sense of shame. Beneath all the boasting and tumult of war, every decent person feels ashamed of this appalling spectacle. During the last war Dr. L. P. Jacks, of Oxford University, wrote, "I cannot get away from the feeling that I am in the presence of some colossal stupidity." Who of us does not feel that now?

Moreover, we blame ourselves for it. We, the democracies that won the last war and sat in places of dominant control, if only we had been resolute when we should have been, and internationally co-operative when we had the chance to be, could have prevented all this. Such self-blame we have heaped upon ourselves. Dr. Carlton J. Hayes, professor of history at Columbia University, has put the matter up to the United States with shocking bluntness: "We did our part to win the First World War, and then we did more than our part to lose the peace. Victimized by a narrow and selfish nationalism, whose other name has been "isolation," we insisted on our rights in 1920 and spurned our duties. We were first to repudiate the League of Nations which our own President had fashioned, and we thus set the pace for its later floutings by other countries." I wonder if ever before great nations have been so ashamed of themselves as we have been.

The final touch of poignancy is added to our penitence when we face the outcome now—our sons, who are not old enough to have been responsible for the world's tragedy, bearing upon their young lives its fearful consequence, the guilt of the world once more falling on the innocent. I, for one, cannot see what is happening to the youth of our time without crying for myself and my generation, "God be merciful to me, a sinner!" There is good reason why the sense of shame is a prevalent emotion among decent folk today.

You might expect a preacher to be pleased with this fact. Is it not one of the preacher's major tasks to get people to be penitent? Certainly, having often tried to do that, I am surprised to find myself now regarding with deep anxiety this powerful, prevalent sense of shame. Yet today an evident fact confronts us: being ashamed of oneself does not necessarily serve a good end but can be one of the most debilitating of human experiences, sapping strength, deflating faith and hope, leaving us enfeebled by a sense of our own guilt so that we are good for nothing.

Put yourself, for example, into the place of that Prodigal Son in the Far Country. When his evil courses ended among the swine, we may be sure he was ashamed of himself. But ask any psychiatrist what that experience might easily have done to him and you will get a long list of the fearful consequences of the guilt complex. Suicides' graves and mental hospitals fill up with the victims of self-reproach, and beaten souls drag out discouraged years because they have done something that makes them unutterably ashamed. There is more to the story of that Prodigal's return than the sense of guilt. For years preachers have told us that he came home because he was ashamed of himself, but he might have been ashamed of himself until all his emotions were one mass of contrition, and yet never have come home at all, but stayed there, whipped and beaten, a disintegrated soul. The crux of the matter was the way he handled his powerful disgust with himself, getting out of it not its disheartenment but its stimulus. Listen to Jesus' account: "When he came to himself he said, How many hired servants of my father's have bread enough and to spare, and I perish here with hunger! I will arise and go." So! There was a healthy, positive, constructive use of the sense of shame that instead of leaving him a yielding mass of self-disgust, waked him up as he never had been waked up before, to say, "I will arise and go."

What a mistake we preachers commonly make about this matter! We preach as though there were only two kinds of people, the impenitent and the penitent. There are the impenitent—proud, self-satisfied, like the Prodigal's elder brother, boasting to his father an impossible thing, "I never transgressed a commandment of thine"—and we talk as though, if only we could get such folk to be contritely ashamed of themselves, that would solve the problem. The fact is, however, that multitudes of people are already so disgusted with themselves that their hearts are eaten out by their sense of failure. There are not two kinds of people but three. First, the impenitent, proud, conceited, self-satisfied; second, the penitent, so crushed and enfeebled by their contrite self-reproach that they go all to pieces and are good for nothing; third, people like the Prodigal, who hate themselves for their failure but find in that sense of shame the most stimulating experience of their lives, and, standing up even in the midst of their swine pasture, cry, "I will arise and go."

This truth has both personal and social significance today, and we may help ourselves to understand it by backing off for a moment from our individual problems and thinking of our public attitudes. We of the democracies are ashamed of ourselves, and we had better be. Mr. Wendell Willkie has said that in the thirteen lands he visited on his trip around the world he found four major facts, and one of them was this: "They all doubt the readiness of the leading democracies . . . to stand up and be counted upon for the freedom of others after the war is over." They have reason to doubt. Today one of Japan's mightiest resources, that may turn out to be stronger even than her armies, is the deep-seated conviction among the teeming millions of Asia that the white race cannot be trusted to treat the colored races with equity. Why should they think otherwise? We, the democracies, are likely to reap a terrific harvest from our racial sins.

Moreover, the whole world knows how little democracy means to us when it comes to the racial line within our own nation. I get letters from people in this city filled with anti-Semitic hatred so dreadful that Hitler himself could hardly improve upon it. In one of our states today there is a large and lovely lake, and on that lake a camp including both white and colored soldiers, equally ready to die for their country. A friend of mine has seen ten thousand of those soldiers swimming at one time in that lake, but no Negro was among them. Owing to local prejudice, the military authorities dare not allow a colored man to enter the water. Far from being an isolated phenomenon, this is symbolic of an intolerable situation affecting nearly one-tenth of the population of the United States. No section of the country is free from blame. Whether it be Jim Crow segregation, the closing of hotels and restaurants to Negroes, the refusal to address them as Mr. or Miss or Mrs., accosting them only by their given names, the denial to them of equality before the law, at the ballot box, and in educational opportunity, or the restriction of their employment to certain narrow fields regardless of their abilities, North and South alike we must rethink our attitude toward the Negro if we are not to make a farce of our democracy. And nowhere is this more true than in our churches where often it is sheer hypocrisy to read from the New Testament, "There cannot be Greek and Jew, circumcision and uncircumcision, barbarian, Scythian, bondman, freeman; but Christ is all, and in all."

We preachers have had a strange experience in this war. Just as soon as the war broke, alike from the church press and from the lips of church leaders the message came that war always begets pride—our side all right and the other side all wrong—and that whatever else the church should do she ought to preach penitence, humility, the contrite recognition of our own sins. Well, we started in on that. Let the democracies be penitent, we said; they won the last war; they sat in the places of power; they could have prevented all this; they ought to be ashamed. Now, however, we wake up to see that while all that is true, with multitudes of thoughtful, sensitive, decent people, that is not where the real trouble lies. We are ashamed. We are burdened by the sense of guilt and failure, and out of that powerful mood of self-condemnation comes often not good but evil—broken morale; lost faith in democracy; confused ethical judgments as though to say, What is the difference anyway between democracy and nazism; cynicism about the great ideas on which democracy is based; and in general an inner weakening of faith and hope and resolution.

So today I change the tune. If anybody here is proud of democracy's record in the last twenty-five years, I leave him to his own devices. But to the rest of us who are humiliated and contrite a vital message comes from the story of the Prodigal. The powerful sense of shame prevalent today is going to do something to us, good or bad, and almost everything depends on which it does. Let us, at least, in our own lives, be spurred by our self-reproach to say, "I will arise." After all, there is a difference between the dreadful things the Nazis do *in accordance with* their philosophy and the dreadful things we do *against* our philosophy. We ought to be ashamed —ashamed of ourselves but not of the basic ideas of democracy. This time of self-reproach can be the most awakening era democracy ever had. It had better be! We white folk have reached the end of the road we have been traveling, professing the democratic faith but denying its substantial meaning in our dealing with colored peoples, whether in our imperialistic subjection of whole nations, like India, or in our denial of elementary civic rights within our own borders, as in the United States, where poll tax laws shut millions of Negroes from the ballot box.

As for war, how idiotic sound now the [words of] Edmund Burke: "The mode of civilized war whic[h more than any]thing else has distinguished the Christ[ian World]"! War has now become the chief enemy of eve[rything ci]vilization stands for and desires, and especially the [cause of democ]racy, and we, the democracies, although [we have] been the dominant power in the world, have faile[d to build] a world organization that alone can prevent it. [We ough]t to be ashamed; it will be mankind's salvation th[at we are] ashamed, if only we make some positive, constructi[ve use of] our contrition, saying, with the Prodigal in his [far pa]sture, "I will arise and go."

If, however, this high use of the sense o[f shame i]s going to be effective in our public attitudes, we sha[ll have to] start with it in our individual lives, and to that end [let us see] now how commonly this powerful emotion of self-reproach, personally experienced, serves no good purpose. Who has not met these people I shall now describe?

Here is one man. He has been guilty of moral failure, and as Victor Hugo said, remorse, like a tide out of the great deep, pours up around his shores. He is thoroughly ashamed and, like a whipped dog, shrinks from looking anybody in the face. One can readily imagine the Prodigal Son in the Far Country feeling and acting like that.

Here is another man. He has made a mess of things and his sense of guilt hurts so that he cannot stand it thus to blame himself; so he blames others. He shoulders off the responsibility for his failure on circumstance, heredity, other people, anything to get rid of his crushing self-reproach. So he grows bitter and cynical because he really is ashamed. Anyone can imagine the Prodigal Son feeling and acting like that.

Here is another man. He has done wrong. He is so ashamed that he thinks he is a complete failure, and accepting that idea finds in it a comforting relief. After all, if a man is a complete

[85]

failure he need not expect anything of himself. That lets him off; it is a grand excuse; he need not even try any more. One can easily imagine the Prodigal Son feeling like that.

Here is another man. He has sinned and he is sorry for it. He gets the idea that thus being sorry is a kind of recompense, as though that alone were in itself a way of making up for the wrong done, a pious compensation to God and man for his mistake. So he wallows in feeling sorry, lives in a morass of emotional self-reproach that never leads anywhere. Anyone can imagine the Prodigal feeling like that.

That is to say, one of the most indispensable and powerful emotions of the human heart—the sense of moral shame—is commonly wasted. But it is a tragedy to waste it. The sense of shame is so agonizing, so much the most tormenting experience we know, that to squander it so that nothing positive and constructive comes out of it is an appalling failure. The great characters of history have sprung from its noble uses. From Paul and Augustine on, what amazing consequences have come from its constructive handling! And now we, facing within ourselves this invaluable experience, twist it to ignoble uses and squander it on futile outcomes. I am thinking today especially of some young man or woman shamed by moral failure. That contrition of yours can be one of the most valuable experiences you ever faced, the very pistol shot, as it were, that will start you off on a fresh course, saying, "I will arise."

To help make possible such constructive response to shame instead of its futile squandering, consider one basic fact suggested by the story of the Prodigal. Moral failure can be turned to positive good. We constantly teach that about trouble. Trouble, we say, is dreadful, but strong souls turn it to such good account that from it come the noblest elements in their character. Disaster may be a deep, dark mine, but men dig precious metal from it. How often have we said here, No calamity—no courage; no hardship—no hardihood; no stress

—no strength; no suffering—no sympathy; no cross—no Christ. One of the major businesses of life is thus to transmute adversity into strength of character.

Too seldom do we hear that same thing said about moral failure. The prevalent teaching about that is negative. Moral failure is sin; it will be inexorably punished; one should be ashamed of it and turn from it, and by God's grace he may be forgiven for it. When all that is said, however, the dreadful experience of moral failure remains, unredeemed to any positive, fruitful outcome.

I cannot so picture that Prodigal when he got home. I suspect that all the rest of his days he had an understanding sympathy with boys, a sensitive touch, so that he knew just where to lay his fingers on a young man's problem; an appreciation of moral rectitude and integrity of character so that, when he spoke of it, his words had a moving accent; and a personal humility that made tempted souls turn naturally to him for help. I suspect that out of that dark mine of his moral failure he dug precious metal. No one knew better than the Prodigal the truth in our common teaching about sin—that it is dreadful, that it is punished pitilessly, that one should be abysmally ashamed of it, and that there is no other way out except to be forgiven. But the Prodigal, I suspect, went a step further —it is a stimulating step to take—and saw that one need not waste all that agonizing experience, but can capitalize it, transmute it into insight, wisdom, character, usefulness.

We are being told on every side today not to waste anything. I am saying now to someone here, Do not waste your moral failure; it is deplorable, but don't waste it; it need not be a total loss; not only can you escape from it but you can make use of it. The Apostle Paul himself started as a persecutor of the church. I never read his thirteenth chapter of I Corinthians on love without seeing those blood-stained hands of his writing it. That violence of his against the Christians was an awful sin; he suffered agony about it but he learned

something from it so profound and moving that when h
about the opposite of violence, love, he said somethin
forgettable that no ordinary man could ever have said.
moral failure was not wasted.

If someone protests that it is dangerous doctrine to say
that sin can be put to good uses, I answer, No! Just because
trouble can be used to great ends nobody goes out looking
for it, and just because sin can be transmuted into gain, no
one will plunge into it. To make a huge blunder, to land in
a Far Country, to suffer shame's agony, and then to have to
come back again, saying, "I am no more worthy to be called
thy son"—no man in his senses will go out looking for that.
But when trouble and moral failure come—and they do come
to all of us—don't waste them! The greatest characters of history have been, as it were, born out of the travail of the sense
of shame.

There is no hope for the world if we fail to put into practice
now this basic truth. The ultimate shame of our dominant
democracies will not be that up to date we have failed, but
that, having failed, we learned nothing from our failure, and,
discouraged by our shame, stayed in the swine pasture where
our sins have landed us. Our posterity will not curse us, but
will positively glory in the remembrance of us, if, stabbed wide
awake, instructed and stimulated by our abysmal stupidities
and iniquities, we now, like the Prodigal, arise and go.

As for our personal lives, we are all in some degree like
that youth in the Far Country. He was not one self but two—
a Prodigal and a son. He was both, and everything depended
on which of the two he thought he really was. Had he thought
of himself as really a Prodigal he would have stayed there,
sunk in shame. But one day something happened in him that
could happen here now. Deep within himself he said to himself,
even there amid the swine, I am really a son; underneath all
this moral failure, that is what I really am: "I will arise and
go to my father."

Christianity Not a Form But a Force

I N THE second letter to Timothy is a description of a formal, conventional Christian, that our standard versions render thus: "Holding a form of godliness, but having denied the power thereof." Dr. Moffatt, however, uses more pungent language: "Though they keep up a form of religion, they will have nothing to do with it as a force."

That describes many people. In the United States today there are between fifty and sixty million members of Christian churches, and were Christ's faith and way of life a vital force in anything like that number, the condition of this country would be far better than it is. Gratefully appreciating the genuine faith and character in our churches, yet when one surveys the scene as a whole, one understands the lines of a modern poet about our worshiping congregations:

> They do it every Sunday,
> They'll be all right on Monday;
> It's just a little habit they've acquired.

This conventional acceptance of religion as a form, with no corresponding experience of it as a force, is easily understandable. Of American religion two things can be said. First, we are not pagans, utterly untouched by the influence of the Christian heritage. Rather, the long-accumulated effect of Christian teaching, mediated in endless ways—through our literature, our family traditions, and our social customs—has become part and parcel of us, so that we know in general what the Christian faith is all about. Second, we are not, on the whole, antagonistic to Christianity, but rather, respectful and even reverent toward it and grateful that it is here. While, however, the overwhelming proportion of us are thus neither pagan in our ignorance of Christianity nor atheistic in our opposition to it, multitudes of us, vaguely acquiescent in it, complacent toward it, and occasionally observant of its outward expressions, fulfill exactly the description of our text: We have a form of religion but have nothing to do with it as a force. As Stanley Jones put it, inoculated with a mild form of Christianity, we have become immune to the genuine article.

Today, however, this kind of nebulous, conventional Christianity confronts a challenge that concerns us all, for the antichristian attack that has plunged the whole world into blood and tears is not a form but a force. What a force it is— vital, dynamic, sacrificial, terrific, massing millions behind an antichristian philosophy and way of life! My friends, we cannot meet a force with a form. It takes a dynamic force to conquer a dynamic force.

All great faiths confront now this demand for reality: democracy, for example. Of how many of us, conventional believers in democracy and inheritors of its political routine, is it true that though we have kept up the form of democracy, we have had all too little to do with it as a force? Intellectually acquiescent in its theories without being personally dedicated to see that it really works, vaguely believing in it in general but not taking it in earnest as a way of living seven days a week, consenting to it as an Election Day technique but not experiencing it as a spirit that must inform all our social, economic, and racial relationships—alas, democracy too has been to multitudes of us not a force but a form! And now totalitarianism, prodigiously powerful, is let loose in the world, and if, in the long run, democracy is going to win, it must become in the hearts of millions of us no longer a conventionality but a reality.

Well, that is true of Christianity. Miss Mildred McAfee says: "Of Wellesley students, 98.8 per cent enter college with some church affiliation. Approximately the same proportion are essentially ignorant of the history and literature of the religious tradition to which they claim allegiance." She ought to know—she is the President of Wellesley College. But if anything remotely like that is true, Christianity is in peril, for this is a generation when the whole earth has become a battlefield where not forms but dynamic forces are contending.

Consider, for one thing, that Christianity becomes vital in our lives when it meets a deep and consciously felt need. In any realm the sense of reality is proportionate to our awareness of need. No one could convince us that food is a mere form—we need it. No one could persuade us that inventive science or the physician's skill is a mere form—they meet urgent wants.

One major reason why Christianity has been to many only a conventionality is that they have felt no crucial necessity that only Christianity could meet. Doubtless you read in the papers recently the amazing story of a group of American fliers, forced down on a South Sea island, who spent weeks with the natives there before they could escape. These natives had been under the influence of missionaries and were Christians; and believe it or not those American boys say that, persuaded by those South Sea islanders, they became Christians there, and returning, they announce for the world to hear that as for them they too are Christians now. One's first reaction is to say, Surely those American boys, brought up in our schools and very probably in our churches, had heard all about Christianity before. Why, on a South Sea island, under the influence of converted natives, should it cease being to them a form and become a force? To which, of course, the answer is that it takes more than seed to make a crop—it takes soil. And when it comes to planting the gospel, a necessary ingredient of the soil is a sense of moral and spiritual need. There on a South Sea island those young men faced a situation that opened up in them a profound and conscious want that they discovered Christ's faith and way of life could fill.

Though it be in less dramatic ways, that kind of experience is being called for among all of us. Personally and socially·we are up against destructive forces. Discouragement is a force; pessimism, fear, disillusionment, cynicism assail our souls with a power, before which only a resistant power can stand. And as for moral life in these days of separated families and disintegrated human relationships, passion and devil-may-care recklessness of decent standards threaten even those who had thought themselves most safe. What if in some of us a deep and conscious need should reveal for the first time that Christ, his faith about life, his way of living life, his power for sustaining life, is food for our hunger, water for our thirst, medicine for our sickness, and power to carry on—not a form, but a force!

As for the world at large, I ask you—do you want antichrist to win? No preacher need paint a fancy picture of him now. We can see him—antichrist—the embodied exhibition of godless philosophies of life and ways of living. Do we like him? If we do not, Christianity must become a force in this world, and at that point there is no passing of the buck to some abstraction or even to the church. That is up to you and me, millions of us, to whom the Christian faith ceases to be a form and becomes dynamically real.

Consider further that any religion, Christianity in particular, becomes a force not only when in general we wake up to our need of it but when it is personally experienced as a source of inward power. The saddest failure of the church is not hypocrisy. I bear witness after many years in the ministry that I have run into very little conscious, deliberate hypocrisy. The saddest failure of the church is seen in men and women like one member of a New York City parish who said to his minister, "I have been a church member since I was baptized twenty-five years ago. Why has nothing vital happened to me in all that time?" He knew about Christianity; he believed it; he had been observant of its customs and a servant of its institutions, but after twenty-five years it looked to him more and more like a form, because he never had gone down to its depths where the power of God becomes a reliable resource in daily living. I have lived with church members too long not to know that there are some such here today.

When we think about conversion we commonly think of prodigals suddenly turning homeward, of drunkards recovered from their alcoholism, and debauchees transformed by the renewing of their minds. Such miracles of personal renovation do take place, but some of the most notable conversions are of another kind—church members who never have doubted Christianity, who have for years been acquiescent in it and observant of its outward expression, who suddenly make a great discovery—it works! It actually works! When translated into the terms of daily life as a resource of inward power, overcoming fear, reinforcing courage, making one an adequate personality equipped for life, able to do what one ought to do and to endure what one must stand, it works. It is not simply creed but personal power, not a form but a force! May God grant some such conversion here today!

A letter recently came from one of our members in Sicily. When he was here a few months ago he was a musician, a promising young composer. Now he is a captain at the front. They have had no chaplain with his unit and he has made himself responsible for the spiritual needs of his men. Among other things he writes this: "These boys are very 'practical' about their religion. That is, they actually look to it for strength to bear their immediate problems." Well, I should say so! Put men into the situation that war confronts them with and of what use is religion as a form? One of two things you do with religion then: either you discard it as useless or else you rediscover it as an inner secret of personal power.

It is not war alone, however, that confronts us with that

choice. Ordinary life can be tragic, too, and soon or late failure, disaster, illness, grief, fall on every life, and men and women do one of two things with this Christianity they have been mildly acquiescent in: either they throw it away as an empty conventionality or else they rediscover it as personal power. Some here today are facing that choice. You have kept up religion as a form, but you have reached the end of that road. No form is adequate now. Far from being at Christianity's end, however, this might be for you its great beginning. "Strengthened with might by God's Spirit in the inner man"—that is Christianity, not a form but a force!

Come further now and see that Christianity becomes a dynamic reality in life not only when we wake up to our need of it and discover in it a resource of personal power but when we are convinced that its basic faiths are everlastingly true. One of the supreme hours in human experience arrives when a man gets his eye on something concerning which he is persuaded that it is the eternal truth, and so finds himself not so much possessing something as being possessed by something to which his mind and heart belong. That is religion—not keeping up a form but being captured by a truth concerning which one is sure that it is everlastingly so!

So far as the basic propositions of the Christian gospel are concerned, I never found that experience more real than now. Part of the reason, I doubt not, is the clarity and horror with which the alternative propositions are now presented—incarnate antichristianity in full operation. When men tell us now that Christianity has broken down, the answer leaps up out of this appalling situation. Is it Christianity that has proved false? Is it not the alternatives to Christianity that threaten the world and commit assault and battery on everything most worth our care?

Take even the realm where the Christian way of life is most beset with difficulty now—the conflict between violence and goodwill as the sovereign power and ultimate organizer of the world. Antichristianity says that only violence can fill the bill, that war is the law of life, that might makes right,

> That they should take, who have the power,
> And they should keep who can.

Christianity calls that false, and affirms something else altogether as true, namely, that no salvation is possible on earth save in goodwill—intelligent, constructive, creative goodwill, too strong to be swamped by hatred, too persistent to be tired out by wrong, too hardheaded to be taken advantage of by deceivers, too world-wide to be hemmed in by prejudice. There is the world's choice today, Christ versus antichrist, and as for me I am convinced that Christ is everlastingly right.

If someone says, But see how futile goodwill is to meet the necessities of such an hour as this and put out the conflagration of our time, I answer, When upon a great fire a few buckets of water are thrown and the fire still rages, would you argue that therefore water is of no avail in quenching fire? My friend, the fact remains that water can put out fire—only you must have enough of it intelligently applied. A few buckets will not do, and their inadequacy proves nothing. So, despite the failure of our little, partial, hesitant experimentations with organized goodwill, the abiding, long-range truth is that man's salvation lies there alone, where the Master says it lies—in the increase of patient, persistent, undiscourageable, intelligent, organized goodwill.

To be gripped by such convictions makes Christianity not a form but a force. May God multiply the number of those who so see it! If someone says that these are hard days in which so to believe in Christ's way of life, I remind you that our text came out of hard days, too. Read the context and see: "Mark this, there are hard times coming in the last days. For men will be selfish, fond of money, boastful, haughty, abusive, disobedient to their parents, ungrateful, irreverent, callous, relentless, scurrilous, dissolute, and savage; they will hate goodness, they will be treacherous, reckless and conceited, preferring pleasure to God"—that is the context. So what? All the more, says the text, because this is the situation, make Christianity not a form but a force.

Finally, consider that Christianity becomes a dynamic power in life when it becomes a strong, organized, devoted fellowship. All through this sermon, I doubt not, some have been thinking of the church, its worship, its rituals, its creeds, its conventional observances, as the very quintessence of formal religion. Well, the church can be that—that is the church's danger as it is the danger of all institutions—but the church need not be that. The forces of evil in this world are too strong to be met by isolated individuals. Organized evil must be met by an organized fellowship of men and women, jointly devoted to nobler ends, and that the church can be. Moreover, with all its appalling failures, the church has not altogether missed being that. It is Professor Shotwell of Columbia University, writing as a historian, who says: "Religion moves, vast and potent, in the world to-day. One must be blind, indeed, not to see the evidences of its power in both the structure and the movement of our modern world."

Indeed, in seeming contradiction to what we have been saying, let us for a moment celebrate the function of the church as a preserver of Christianity's forms. A rememberable story concerns the College of William and Mary in Virginia. Damaged and closed during the Civil War and precariously reopened afterward, it faced later the necessity of another suspension which lasted seven years. But "every morning," we read, "during those seven barren years President Ewell rang the chapel bell. There were no students; the faculty had disappeared; and rain seeped though the leaky roofs of the desolate buildings. But President Ewell still rang the bell." See! He was keeping up the form, as though to say, Despite immediate disaster, the intellectual life will come back again and fill these empty halls with reality once more and be a vital and dynamic power. More than once in history the church has done that. All that the gospel stood for seemed lost—men deserted it and antagonistic forces ruled the world —but still the church kept ringing the bell. In our time we may have to do that again.

Such a barren time, however, is not inevitable if now enough of us make our Christianity a force. Men and women who feel deeply the need of Christianity, who have discovered it as a resource of personal power in their own lives, who believe that its basic faiths are everlastingly true, and who bind themselves together in a fellowship to make it actually work in this world—the times cry out for such.

Our World Confronts a Child

AMID the violent events of this warring world we need as wide horizons around our thinking as we can get. To see the eternal surrounding the temporal, the universal encompassing the local, helps to keep us steady and wise. So with good reason we turn repeatedly for reassurance to our Christian faith in God. This morning, however, in our quest for something universal to rest our eyes on we start not with the greatest of all facts, God, but with one of the smallest of all facts, a little child. As a scientist finds eternal truth not simply with a telescope but with a microscope, so we today seek wisdom by looking at a child.

In an Old Testament story, narrated in the thirteenth chapter of the Book of Judges, a man named Manoah and his wife were visited by an angel of the Lord who told them they were going to have a son, and Manoah's response was a prayer that I should suppose would find an echo in every sensitive heart today. Manoah entreated the Lord and said, "Oh, Lord, I pray thee, let the man of God whom thou didst send come again unto us, and teach us what we shall do unto the child that shall be born." That prayer surely belongs to us. What are we, the nations of the world, going to do to the children that shall be born?

Such a prayer does lift our thought to a vantage point from which the wild events of these times are seen in a fresh perspective. Something universal is in a little child. A newborn babe is not yet a German or a Japanese or a Russian or an American; he is a new piece of humanity in whom not the particulars that divide us but the universals that unite us are incarnate. In the volcanic ashes of Pompeii the excavators found the skeleton of a deformed child with his mother's arm around him. The mother's jewelry, the archaeologists say, reveal her to have been a member of the wealthy class, who must have had time to save herself as did the others of her class in that neighborhood. So, she must have gone back to rescue her crippled boy, and through all the centuries since, her arm has been beneath the child she died to save. Now of what race or of what nation were that mother and child? Who knows or cares? Not something local but something universal is represented in that ancient scene.

If only all men believed in God, we say, we would have a universal outlook from which we could start to build a better world—one God, all men his children, all mankind one family. But multitudes do not really believe in God, and many more who do, do not draw that logical conclusion; and so once more, on both sides of a bloody battle line, men pray to the same God to destroy their enemies. Yet all the time one thing does unite us, a universal bond overpassing race and nation—our care for our children, a moving passion stronger than the love of money or the fear of death, that makes all mankind akin. What if in this violent age, when in another war we are starving the bodies, blasting the minds, twisting the characters, and wrecking the prospects of millions of little children, we could be lifted to see the world from the vantage point of this universal fact! Ages have gone since Manoah lived, but on one matter he is as contemporary as today's New York *Times*: "Oh, Lord, I pray thee, . . . teach us what we shall do unto the child that shall be born."

Consider, then, some consequences that would follow if we really looked at the world from that standpoint. The first is clear: we would be penitent. This is the Lenten season, dedicated to penitence, but it is of small use merely to urge ourselves to repent. Today we are urging ourselves not so much to repent as to face the facts and see if we possibly can avoid penitence. The chairman of the Greek Red Cross reports that when Greece was first attacked there were three hundred thousand little children in Athens and the Piraeus. Today 110,000 of them are dead of starvation and epidemics. A neutral observer in Greece describes conditions there as Dante's Inferno—88 per cent mortality in one typical children's hospital. We say that Hitler did it. Yes, he did! But in a real sense we did it, too—we, the nations who at the close of the last war had the greatest opportunity in history, and muffed it; and now today some of the same old voices rise that caused that colossal failure then, and if they prevail will cause its like again. Long ago Jesus put a little child in the midst of his disciples. If only we could put a child again in the midst of the world's statesmen! What happens to us older folk does not matter so much; but the children that shall be born—can we not create a more decent world for them? That is not a sentimental matter but the supreme issue on earth today. That is what the best of our youths who are going out to fight think they are fighting for.

One of the first great prophets against war in human history was Euripides, the Greek dramatist, and in his drama, *The Trojan Women*, first performed in Athens in 416 B.C., he made the same appeal that we are making now. What was his symbol of war—a panoplied soldier armed to the teeth and bristling with courage? No, nothing like that! He brought on the scene as his ultimate symbol of war a solitary old woman with a dead baby in her arms. Call Euripides a pagan if we will, he knew enough when thinking of war to put a little child "in the midst of them." What would he say now about our war, with its mass starvation and its bombing of civilian populations, bringing the whole ictus and tragedy of war to bear on the one thing that all of us alike—Germans and Japanese, Russians and Chinese, British and Americans —care most about, our children? This situation is indeed, as Prime Minister Churchill himself called it, "hideous and fantastic."

All this becomes desperately urgent when we think of the

post-war world. Victory and freedom—how we thrill to the words! But victory will confront us with the weightiest responsibility that ever has rested on any generation in history. Are we going to be worthy of it when we get it? And the criterion of that is what we shall do to the child that shall be born.

Another consequence sure to follow our viewing of the world from this standpoint would be a practical solution to the bitterly debated problem, whether we should love or hate our enemies. On one side, Christians try desperately even in wartime to cling to the Sermon on the Mount and love their enemies; on the other side, tougher men say, What do you mean, loving foes we are going out to kill; let us be honest and say frankly that to kill effectively we must hate heartily.

Into the midst of this controversy I venture to interject a simple proposition: We cannot hate a baby. No! Japanese or German, Russian, French or Italian, British or American— we cannot hate a baby. Or if we can, then we are as bad as the worst we fight against and our souls are damned within us.

The other evening in Madison Square Garden Madame Chiang Kai-shek said this: "There must be no bitterness in the reconstructed world. No matter what we have undergone and suffered, we must try to forgive those who injured us and remember only the lesson gained thereby." Madame Chiang has been criticized for that, as though we Americans were in any position to teach her what dreadful things the Japanese can do. What did she mean, then? Softness toward the Japanese military party? Of course not! A policy of weak appeasement? Of course not! Madame Chiang is a wise, courageous statesman, with a long look and a constructive purpose. She knows, if anybody does, that stern measures will be needed in this war's settlement, but alike her statesmanship and her Christianity agree that we can get nowhere in the building of a better world by hating whole peoples.

We had better not let such mass hatred get started in this

country. Our friend Walter Russell Bowie is right in saying that hatred is like alcoholism. When that really gets hold of a man, he will drink anything—whisky, gin, and at last if nothing else is handy, wood alcohol. So let mass hatred get started, and when its first object is disposed of, it will go on to find another. The furious haters of Japs and Germans, when those special enemies are no longer a problem, will not stop hating. Their hatred will still be in them like a thirst, demanding other satisfaction, and plenty of demagogues will be here to turn it to other groups—Jews, Negroes, Catholics, Protestants, what you will. Hatred is social poison.

This would be true even if we forgot the innocent children of our enemies, with whom our innocent children must grow up and live together in the post-war world. In England when the war was young, at one training center they started a deliberate process of fomenting hatred among the troops, and when the high command heard of it they cracked down on it with a statement that makes one proud of the British. Said General Paget in an official announcement: "Such an attitude of hate is foreign to the British temperament, and any attempt to produce it by artificial stimulus during training is bound to fail, as it did in the last war. Officers and NCO's must be made to realize the difference between the building up of this artificial hate and the building of a true offensive spirit combined with the will power which will not recognize defeat." So! Does a policeman have to froth at the mouth with hatred against the people he arrests? To folk who sit comfortably at home here writing ferocious articles filled with the ballyhoo of hatred, I commend the spirit of the best of our fighting men themselves, like General Paget.

This saner attitude, free from the emotional distortion of furious passion, becomes inevitable when one thinks about the children. Madame Chiang, I suspect, was thinking of them—Chinese children and Japanese children, not to blame for this catastrophe, facing in a new generation the necessity of living together one way or another. That is the world's real problem, and hate is no solution. Once get into the center of our minds the question that is really central: what shall we do to the children that shall be born, and hatred is shown up for what it is—both ethical poison and political folly. Never in the world's history did the Sermon on the Mount make better sense than it does today.

A further consequence bound to follow our looking at the world from the vantage point of a little child is plain—the determination, namely, even in the midst of war, to do everything we can to save the children.

There is in this city now a fifteen-year-old girl, Marianne Benjamin by name, who three years ago escaped from Nazi Germany a frightened, crushed, humiliated child. A few weeks ago, pretty, happy, black-haired, brown-eyed Marianne received the Rebecca Elsberg Memorial Scholarship, one of the most coveted awards of our city schools. She had led her class during 1942. In a special ceremony, we read, held in the office of the superintendent of schools, Marianne, who not long ago could not speak a word of English, and could hardly look you in the eye, was honored by the school officials as having made one of the best scholastic records in the city despite personal and social handicaps. Well, do you know any test of a civilization that goes deeper or includes a wider scope than the question whether or not that kind of thing that happened to Marianne can happen to a child?

Obviously we are dealing here with one of Jesus' central teachings. Again and again he brought great matters to this test of which we are thinking. Once when his disciples were discussing who is greatest in the Kingdom of God, he put a little child in the midst of them, a teachable, humble, open-minded child, rich in the possibilities of growth, and said, "Except ye . . . become as little children, ye shall not enter into the kingdom of heaven." Again, when he talked about what it means to welcome the Divine into our lives, to have

Christ himself as a guest of our souls, he said, "Whoso shall receive one such little child . . . receiveth me." And again, when he spoke of those most damning sins for which no condemnation can be too severe, he said, "Whoso shall cause one of these little ones . . . to stumble, it is profitable for him that a great millstone should be hanged about his neck, and that he should be sunk in the depth of the sea."

In that old tough Roman world how sentimental such teaching must have seemed, but here we are now in America, nearly two thousand years afterwards, knowing well that nothing in our civilization is more indicative of real progress and more promising for the future than the fact that what happened to Marianne Benjamin can happen here.

Well, then, even in the midst of total war, whose most pathetic victims are the children, let us save as many of them as we can! In Washington now, under the governmental agency headed by former Governor Herbert Lehman, plans are afoot to feed the children of the conquered countries in Europe. The necessary funds are available. All we can send are things like vitamins and powdered milk, but these can be sent. They had better be! Help has already begun to reach Greece, and it can reach Belgium and Holland and Norway and the rest. The hope of a new Europe is in those children, but there is no hope in a child who has been starved too long.

As for our own land, we shall be fools indeed if we let the awful necessities of war wreck the agencies that serve the children, break down the restrictions on child labor, or cripple the schools that educate the young, as is dangerously happening in many places in this country now. In this Gargantuan world of titanic forces at war, a little child seems pitifully small, but in all our most intelligent hours we know that he is not. Recall the father of William the Conqueror, starting on crusade to the Holy Land, and before he went, requiring his barons to swear allegiance to his young son. The barons smiled at the child they were pledging their devotion to, but the king said to them, "He is little, but he will grow." So he did, to become William the Conqueror. Well, into what shall our children grow? What kind of conquest will their portion be? That is the central question on earth today.

Surely, then, the sum of our thought is this: seen from the vantage point of a little child, it is war itself that is the great curse. Today as we listen to the radio and read the papers, we hear of clashing armies, vast battles, and all the huge affairs of a world at war. Here, however, in the church of Christ, we remind ourselves of news that never makes the headlines—the obscure, forgotten, unheralded ruin that is falling on the world's children. For war is no longer mainly grown-ups slaying grown-ups. Its central tragedy now, its most fatal curse and hideous consequence is its destruction of the bodies, minds, and souls of little children.

There are two ways of regarding war. First, as the instrument by which we overthrow our enemies, and second, as itself the major enemy that most needs to be overthrown. In wartime the first obsesses our attention. We are absorbed in war as a means of overthrowing our foes. But we shall come to the same futile consequence, and end in the same era of disillusionment that the last war brought unless that second point of view holds its ground in our minds. Think of the children, and war is not simply the means by which we overthrow our enemies; it is itself the enemy that must be overthrown.

As a Christian minister I suppose I ought, in days of strain and tension, to find my strength in God. Well, I do! There are days, however, when like many a believer of old I am tempted to talk rebelliously to him. You made the world, I would say to him, and you can take care of it; do not roll on me the responsibility for this insane business; I am tired and cynical and out of heart, and want to rest. But even when life looks like that, to think of the children gives renewed strength to a decent man. They are worth while; they are the incarnate future tense of mankind; they are the seed corn of the race. The love of children is the one universal bond that across all racial and national lines makes all mankind akin. The co-operative world, organized for peace, that, like the fools we are, we have refused to build for our own sakes, we may be wise enough at last to build for their sakes. So, we will keep the faith and not surrender. We will not let the children down. Still Manoah's prayer shall be our own until its answer comes: "Oh, Lord, . . . teach us what we shall do unto the child that shall be born."

On Being Strongly Tempted To Be Christian

THE word "temptation" is almost universally associated with evil. Say of a man that he is tempted, and the immediate inference is that he is lured to do wrong. Why do we so habitually think and speak as though life's major enticements were thus on the side of sin? That is not the realistic truth about our experience.

I do not mean simply that there are lovely as well as evil things that tempt us—of course there are! Beauty and truth and goodness, great music, great books, great art, inspiring homes and fine friends, causes worth serving, faiths worth believing, hopes worth fulfilling, character worth attaining, and Christ over all, saying, "Follow me"—life with all its evil is full of enticements to good. Such emphasis, however, upon life's lovely and alluring aspects does not reveal in its full dimensions the profound experience we are dealing with. The temptation to be Christian can be not simply lovely but terrific.

The Apostle Paul is an outstanding illustration of this fact. He hated Christianity at first, presided at the death of Stephen, the first Christian martyr, and "breathing threatening and slaughter against the disciples of the Lord," we read, he "laid waste the church." But even then inside Paul something else was going on that we wish we knew the details of. Intelligent man that he was, he could not persecute a movement without trying to understand it, but the more he understood about Christ, and the more he saw of those first Christians whom he was harrying to their death, the more he was tempted, goaded in a direction he hated and had not the slightest intention of moving in. Paul, the persecutor of Christianity, inwardly tempted to be Christian himself—that situation illustrates one of our profoundest experiences. Thus on the Damascus Road, when Paul surrendered his life to Christ, he heard Christ say to him, "Saul, Saul, why persecutest thou me? it is hard for thee to kick against the goad." Ah, Paul, like a stubborn ox, you were being inwardly goaded toward an outcome that seemed to you intolerable! Is not that a true picture of our world today and of some of us in it, and would not Christ be justified in saying to us now, "It is hard for thee to kick against the goad"?

When the Prodigal Son, for example, left home for the Far Country, he was tempted by evil, we say, and fell. To be sure! But when at last he was in the Far Country, draining the dregs of his bitter cup, he was tempted again—this time to go home to his father. There amid the swine that strong allurement now appealed to his reason and tugged at his heart. He fought against it, tried to escape the humiliation of a penitent return, but surrendering at last to a pull he could not resist he turned his face homeward. Thus we do get into places, as Paul did, where we are goaded to be decent, driven, drawn, and coerced to clean up our lives, and in our generation that experience is widespread and deep-seated. For mankind, under the terrific pressure of evil's consequence, is crying out for a new kind of world, a more Christian kind of world, if only to avoid another war! How can even an unbeliever look at our earth now without wishing that we could be at least a little Christian?

Multitudes of people today are thus feeling the pull of the Christian faith and way of life, and this morning I invite you to meet some of them.

Here, for example, is a man who has been so scornful of Christianity that, like Paul at first, told he would ever be a Christian, he would have laughed, and for a good deal the same reason. Paul got his first superficial impression of Christianity from the little struggling church in Jerusalem— from the oddities of its members, their meager intelligence and their small bigotries. He despised them. But then as he tried to understand why this superstition he hated was wielding such growing influence, he made a disturbing discovery—great ideas back there that a man had better think about, and spiritual powers that one could not intelligently laugh at. So Paul, breaking through the superficial crust of Christianity, its petty and often pitiful exhibitions, and facing now what at its profoundest and best it really meant, found himself to his amazement and his horror tempted to be a Christian himself.

That kind of experience is being reduplicated today. The church, with its formal services and sermons, its sometimes pitiful exhibitions of sectarianism and obscurantism, is often not tempting. Macaulay was a good man, but he was off the church. He seldom went and when he did he almost invariably recorded in his diary his disapproval: "A bad sermon as usual," he wrote; and again: "a most detestable sermon"; the best he could say was once when he wrote a grudging approval: "a middling sermon."

Millions of Americans have been thus off the church, and conceiving Christianity itself in terms of such superficial impressions have been scornful of *that,* too. But now many of them are disturbed. They see in our Western world a great tradition of spiritual life, that sprang from the Hebrew prophets and from Christ, that gathered into its growing stream the best that the Greeks thought and the Romans, and in its profoundest insights and noblest qualities draws its inspiration from the life and teaching of Jesus. In that spiritual heritage lies the origin of our ideas of human dignity, of the soul's value, of the rights of conscience before God, of democracy and liberty and human possibility. That is what Christianity is in its greatness—the origin and the continuous conserver of our best spiritual heritage, and today it is being assailed by hostile philosophies and faiths that deny it with such dastardly alternatives that had I never been a Christian, I should be tempted to be one now.

Our choice today is not between belief and unbelief, as we often superficially have thought, but between belief in what Christ stands for and belief in the opposite. Having turned our backs on Christian affirmations about God and man and the soul and the kingdom of righteousness on earth, we now face the consequence—alternative faiths claiming man's allegiance, and with desperate earnestness believed in by millions, so that mankind's choice is not between faith and no faith but between two kinds of faith: God or stark materialism; a spiritually meaningful and purposeful universe or a universe that came from nowhere and in the end means nothing; man a child of the Eternal or a mere accident of the dust; and so at last, organized violence as the natural law of life or organized goodwill as its hope and its possibility. Believe me, when one gets through the superficial crust of Christianity into its depths, it is important!

I am asking someone here today to take at least this first step—to stop thinking of Christianity in terms of its little, petty, superficial exhibitions and to see it in its depths, the great heritage of spiritual faith and life, without which there is no salvation for our race. I want you to be tempted by that, for that ancient scene on the Damascus Road is being reproduced in our generation, Christ saying to us again in our appalling catastrophe: "Saul, Saul, why persecutest thou me? it is hard for thee to kick against the goad."

Here is another man who has been off Christianity because he has thought himself quite self-sufficient. What does he need of Divine help? Let a man, relying upon himself, he thinks, confront life with a strong will and he can handle it.

Thus Paul, at the beginning, was trying to handle his life. God had given the law, he thought; let a man keep it, put his will into it and obey the Commandments! But all the time, deep within Paul was the growing need of inner help if he was indeed to be the kind of person he desired. He talked about that struggle afterwards: "The good which I would I do not: but the evil which I would not, that I practice. . . . Wretched man that I am!" And when, in those first Christians, Paul began to see power released, resources of inner strength from unfathomable wells set free to transform character and make the impossible possible, the goad began to drive him toward Christ. He talked about that afterwards too: "Strengthened with might by his Spirit in the inner man."

Certainly, that experience is being reproduced now. Men today are up against situations where self-sufficiency collapses, pride breaks down, and if there is any power available to see a man through, they know they need it. I am not talking merely about fox-hole religion, the spasmodic cry to God for help in the last ditch. That can turn out to be real and transforming, but much of it is superficial and superstitious—magic, not religion. Discount it, as you will! The sober fact remains that this world, in the fox-holes or out of them, now presents a situation that makes human self-sufficiency look foolish. Tell us there is no God, no righteousness greater than our own, no goodness to rely on for the world's help except the frail goodness, mixed with illimitable evil, that we possess, no power beyond ourselves that makes for righteousness, and human hopes collapse like a house of cards. If I had never been a Christian, and someone now should tell me for the first time about a deep resource of inner power that man can count upon, God's strength available for daily help, I should be tempted to try for it. So one of our Negro friends recently prayed, "O God, help me to understand that you ain't gwine to let nothin' come my way that you and me together can't handle." If I had never heard of that experience before, I should be tempted to try for it now.

Today I wish so to tempt someone here. It is hard enough at any time to be a strong, coherent, steady, well-integrated personality, able to hold together under life's strain and win a spiritual victory, but that is more difficult now than ever. Moreover, there is no use hoping for an outward situation that will make it easier. We are not going to get it, not right away; the world after this war is over will be a mess; and in this situation there are personalities who tempt us, not only saying, like Jesus, "I have overcome the world," but, like him, too, giving us exhibitions of triumphant living, seeing whom we know that our deepest need is to be like that.

One of the strangest marvels in history is the way Jesus has so tempted mankind. Whoever would have dreamed it? Alexander, Caesar, Napoleon—they might tempt us, wishing that we had power like theirs; but Jesus—born in a manger, dying on a cross, his message love, humility, goodwill—why should he so tempt the race? Yet, he is the greatest tempter mankind ever faced. We cannot get rid of him. We picture the tempter as the devil, and the truth in that everybody knows, but still Christ, saying across the centuries, "Follow me," outmatches the devil at his own game, and is the strangest, strongest, most insistent tempter man has ever faced. We say *No* to him, resist him; we kick against the goad and will have none of him, but when we are through he still is there, and in our deepest hours our profoundest selves say, If we could only be like him!

Dr. Rambo, a medical missionary in India, once operated successfully upon an Indian woman who had cataracts upon her eyes, so that at last she left the hospital with her vision restored. As she bade Dr. Rambo farewell she bowed very low and said, "Good-by, God." He expostulated with her, protesting that he was not God, but only one of his humble servants; but she would have none of it, and all the way down the path from the hospital she kept turning back to say, "Good-by, God." There are personalities, Christ above all, who tempt us so. Who of us does not sometimes find it hard to kick against their goad?

A few months ago a Chinese student came to see me. He

had come to America for a scientific education, and now a Doctor of Medicine he was an able and highly trained scientific man. But he was so spiritually hungry that he was being tempted in his extremity to turn to Christ to meet his need. Only, how could he, with his scientific mind, become a Christian? So, drawn to it, he still rebelled against it, and, like Paul at first, was scornful of Christianity even while he came to me wistfully to talk about it. A letter has just come from that man, a medical officer now with one of our units in Australia. He has reproduced in his own way Paul's experience. "Ever grateful for the talk with you," he writes; "Always remember your help. Glad to say that I have found the Something I longed for." So still maintaining unimpaired his scientific rectitude, he has stopped kicking against Christ's goad.

Here is another man who has been off Christianity because he has thought of it as lovely, to be sure, but as utterly impractical idealism; all this talk about love and humility and goodwill, beautiful it may be, but what has that to do with the stern, rough, realistic facts of life? The Christian faith and ethic, he has said, present an impractical ideal. Today, however, he is deeply disturbed. He looks upon a world that, rejecting Christ, has plunged into appalling catastrophe, and a question rises that will not down: Good heavens! Is this thing we are doing now, practical?

We run here upon one of the most stubborn and disturbing facts in history—the way in which repeatedly man's idealism has turned out to be not idealism at all but man's necessity. Universal education, for example, opening the doors of intellectual opportunity to all the boys and girls of a nation, was at first sheer idealism. Save to a few dreamers it seemed incredible. Men doubted its desirability, presented endless arguments against its possibility, and laughed at its proposers as visionaries. But then democracy came, everyone with a vote, and lo, universal education was no longer an ideal but a necessity! No democracy can be run with an illiterate electorate. They must be educated.

So that scene on the Damascus Road represents a universal fact: men kicking against the goad of some ideal decision that they scorn as visionary and call impossible, but that at last turns out to be an absolute necessity. Today our generation as a whole confronts that fact.

The Christian way of life not practical? Very well, but we are engaged now in a wholesale exhibition of the antichristian way of life. Is that practical? Bombing one another's cities to pieces; carefully selecting our best youths and then slaughtering them wholesale; starving a whole generation of little children until they will never be physically or emotionally normal; spending in this country a hundred billion dollars a year on war—look at this antichristian process we are plunged in as some wise observer from a saner planet might see it. Is it practical? Indeed, listen to Adolf Hitler: "After the destruction of Judaism, the extinction of Christian slave morals must follow logically." So, when he has exterminated Judaism, then he will exterminate Christian ethics, too. I ask you honest-to-goodness, does that alternative to the Christian way of life strike you as practical? Upon the contrary, has not the basic ethic of the Sermon on the Mount become a necessity now if we are to have a world fit to live in? At any rate, if I for one had never been a Christian, I should be powerfully tempted to try for it now.

You see, this experience of being tempted to be Christian is not simply lovely. It is stern business. It rests upon the inexorable fact of the reign of law. In an age that boasts of being scientific, why should we forget that whatever men and nations sow they reap? Granted, that the Far Country is tempting at first, but when we get there and land among the swine, that is not tempting. That is where we are now, rejecting the faith and principles of Christ, and choosing their opposites.

To be sure, promiscuous sensuality is tempting, but its consequences are not. Thank God some of us were tempted by a good home! We were born in one. We wanted one for ourselves. Do not tell us now that that choice was visionary idealism!

To be sure, selfishness is tempting, but the results are not.

> The wretch, concentred all in self,
> Living, shall forfeit fair renown,
> And, doubly dying, shall go down
> To the vile dust, from whence he sprung,
> Unwept, unhonored, and unsung.

That is not tempting! But to forget yourself, to belong to something greater than yourself, to lose your life in something worth losing it in, and so to find it—far from being an idealistic dream, that is the law—the basic, realistic law of worthwhile living. The hardest-headed psychiatrists would say of such ethical principles of Jesus that, instead of being ideal, they are the laws of life, as inexorably woven into the structure of the universe as is the law of gravitation. In California there is a monument to a dog who died saving a child from drowning. So! Something deep in us knows that even a dog deserves a monument when he becomes as Christian as that.

As for the world at large, a man who can look on this present situation and call it practical, is mad. What if Christ were the hardheaded realist after all? What if George Bernard Shaw was right: "I am ready to admit that after contemplating the world and human nature for nearly sixty years, I see no way out of the world's misery but the way which would have been found by Christ's will if he had undertaken the work of a modern practical statesman." The voice on the Damascus Road is sounding yet. Ah, Christ, you have been saying it a long time! God help us to hear it now as individuals and as a world before it is too late: "Saul, Saul, why persecutest thou me? it is hard for thee to kick against the goad."

[115]

Starting with Trouble and Ending with Hope

D URING these last few generations, for us of the Western world hope has probably been easier than human beings ever before in history have found it. New discoveries, new inventions, new opportunities, a rising standard of living and all the rest, produced among us a mood of eager expectancy about the future. Who doubted that the present is better than the past and that the future would be better than the present? So, naturally eager for hope, we built a vast structure of optimism. First, we held an optimistic philosophy of history in terms of inevitable progress—all the world evolving by inner necessity toward justice, decency, and peace. Second, we held an optimistic theology about God—a kindly deity who, no matter what we did, would make everything come out all right. Third, we held an optimistic psychology—calling fear imaginary and teaching that all would be well if only we could say with sufficient confidence: "Every day in every way I am getting better and better."

Never before have human beings found hopefulness so easy, but today see that vast and flimsy structure of optimism lying in ruins! Who today escapes the problem of wanting hope, but on every side seeing our optimism proved illusion and the oases we dreamed of only mirages? In my boyhood my father used to sit at the piano and sing the medieval Latin hymn:

> *Dies irae! dies illa,*
> *Solvet saeclum in favilla,*

and I used to think what gloomy pessimists those ancient Christians were to write a hymn like that. But now we might sing it again:

[116]

Day of wrath, O day of mourning,

. . . . . .

Heaven and earth to ashes burning.

If today, then, we are to have hope, we must rethink our way of getting it. So we turn to a strange verse in the fifth chapter of Paul's letter to the Romans as Dr. Moffatt translates it: "Trouble produces endurance, endurance produces character, and character produces hope." That certainly is a way of reaching hopefulness very different from easy-going optimism. Paul begins with trouble; from that he learns endurance; out of that he builds character; and from that he wins hope. Our revised version translates the verse thus: "Tribulation worketh stedfastness; and stedfastness approvedness; and approvedness hope," but that rendering illustrates the frequent inadequacy of the standard versions. In a whole lifetime we would never use the word "approvedness" in such a sense. So all the fresher translations—Moffatt's, Goodspeed's, Weymouth's—agree on rendering Paul's words as we shall use them today. As Weymouth puts it: "Affliction produces endurance; endurance, ripeness of character; ripeness of character, hope."

If ever a man had a right to say a thing like this, Paul had, for this verse is autobiography. The great passage that starts, "Five times received I forty stripes save one. Thrice was I beaten with rods, once was I stoned," is only a partial picture of his tribulations, and as for the world he lived in, no one in his senses would choose to go back from even this troubled time to that. Paul himself started with trouble and ended with hope. An old bookplate bears these words: "Books Once Were Men." Well, this letter to the Romans once was a man.

In the first place, note that this saying of Paul contradicts our prevalent impression that hope is dependent on hopeful circumstances. How common that attitude is—our hopefulness a mere thermometer: things are hopeful so we are hopeful;

things look bad so we lose heart. But Paul, at the very point where things look bad, begins his road to hope.

A man learns endurance, Paul would say, not amid easy situations but in adversity; so, meeting adverse conditions with endurance, a man builds character and becomes the kind of man who confronts hopefully even desperate circumstances. Hope, says Paul, is no mere mood, caught from the favorable aspect of external affairs, but a quality of character called out when most needed—that is, when things look bad. I wonder if Paul knew those great words of Thucydides, the Greek, about men who "dared beyond their strength, hazarded against their judgment, and in extremities were in excellent hope." At any rate, such is the stuff Paul's confidence was made of—trouble, endurance, character, hope.

Look at our American people today—the popular mood, like a weather vane, veering with every change in the wind, now over-optimistic, now over-gloomy—and see how deeply we need this secret of Paul! The noblest exhibitions of un-defeated courage in our generation are arrived at by his route. There is Niemoeller, for example, his nation that he loves and would gladly die for in the hands of a mad policy bound to be its ruin, and he himself in prison. So, the circumstances not so good! But listen to Niemoeller's letter to his parish in Berlin: "Let us thank God that He upholds me as He does and allows no spirit of despair to enter into Cell 448. Let the parish office know that in all ignorance of what is coming I am confident, and that I hope to be ready when I am led along paths which I never would have sought for myself." His hope-fulness is no thermometer. Trouble, endurance, character, and so hope!

On every side the question rises today: What is this war going to do to the world? And that question comes home to each man's doorsill: What is this war going to do to you and me? It is knocking hope clean out of some folk. What is there to look forward to? they say; our optimisms have collapsed, and the stark and horrid facts make a realistic mind cynical about any dreams of decency and peace. As one man cried the other day, "Three sneers for everything and three cheers for nothing!" What people of that kind fail to see is that such hopelessness inside ourselves, springing from the kind of characters we are, is itself the one major thing that will make the world's estate hopeless. We commonly think that hopeless situations make people hopeless, but it is also true that hopeless people make situations hopeless. Give us enough men and women like Paul—trouble producing endurance, endurance character, and character hope—and we could re-make the world.

Note in the second place that Paul's words contradict an-other prevalent idea—that hope is a mere matter of idealism, lovely and comforting, a realm of alluring dreams to which one turns for solace from the realistic facts. That is a common caricature of hope. Upon the contrary, the future tense is one of the most tremendous things that mankind possesses.

One day a youth named Robert Fulton, tired of poling a fishing boat on Conestoga Creek, rigged up a set of paddles to work at the sides of the boat and to be operated by a double hand-crank. The future belonged to that idea so humbly and clumsily begun; all steamships stem out from that hour. That is hope—creative, venturesome, revolutionary. Far from being an easy retreat from the facts, it is the most tremendous transformer of facts that history knows. Every great thing that ever has been done on earth was once a hope.

In times like these it is of vital moment that we go deep into these profounder meanings of life's future tense and what we do with it. We always do something with it. To fill it either with despair or with superficial optimism is fatal—despair ruins us and superficial optimism collapses—but to fill it with the kind of hope reached by Paul's route is creative. Democ-racy itself was so achieved. Once the world was dominated by the political philosophy that Francis I of Austria put into unashamed words: "I require obedient subjects, not enlightened citizens," and democracy was a struggling hope, hard bestead, the faith of a small minority. Always it has been the men and women in whom, amid towering difficulties, the future tense has loomed large and spoken powerfully, who have shaken the world out of its lethargy.

Now, such use of the future tense is an attribute of strong character, as Paul said it was, and we deeply need it. I am ashamed of some Americans today, growing cynical about the possibility of a more decently ordered world and turning back to isolationism or American military imperialism, not daring to try for a really co-operative world organized for peace. Who are we, with our history and our traditions, to lose heart about a better world order, and like hermit crabs crawl back into the outgrown shells of obsolete ancestral social systems and international policies? Why is it that some of the strongest, most confident voices on earth today come from people who like Paul are facing appalling trouble? Listen, for example, to a Danish Christian minister who is not afraid. I should hate to be in his shoes today, preaching in Denmark, but he said recently in a public address in Copenhagen: "We are not allowed to discuss politics here . . . but still I want to tell you that I would rather die with the Jews than live in company with Nazis. If there are any of you who have not understood what I said, I'll gladly repeat it." So, trouble produces endurance, and endurance character, and character hope.

Optimism can be cheap, but an undefeated forward look, like that Danish minister's, to a world characterized by such things as interracial decency and equality, is not cheap. See what elements of character go into it: courage that does not know when it is beaten; venturesomeness as real as in those who pioneer new lands; spiritual pugnacity, a militant determination that, as Jesus said, comes to "cast fire upon the earth" to destroy old and evil things; and persistence that in the service of creative undertakings keeps everlastingly saying, as Emerson said once, "Never mind the ridicule, never mind the defeat; up again, old heart! . . . there is victory yet for all justice." Give us enough such hope, rooted in such character, and the impossible is possible.

All this, however, if we went no further, would be an incomplete presentation of Paul's confidence. So far we have moved altogether on the human plane. Real hope, we have said, is no happy mood borrowed from fortunate situations, nor is it a lotus land of comfortable escape from ugly facts. Real hope, we have said, is an attribute of strong character, the daring, venturesome attack of uncontented souls determined to create something new on earth. But now the question rises, How does a man get that way? What backing and resource is there that can sustain such a courageous attitude despite hell and high water? So we are reminded that we have not yet completed our text, for it ends thus: "A hope which never disappoints us, since God's love floods our hearts through the holy Spirit which has been given to us." Paul, that is, believed something, not simply about what ought to be or might be but about what *is*, an everlasting truth about the nature of this universe: this is God's world, and that being so, it is never hopeless.

Many today looking on this bloody shambles of a world find it harder to believe in God than they have ever found it before. Our friend Maude Royden, of England, however, is on the truer track when she says: "If this war had not occurred, I would have found it hard to believe in God." Just so! If this is God's world, it is morally law-abiding, and in such a world we, the nations, broke all the conditions that make peace possible, and fulfilled all the conditions that make war inevitable. This agony we suffer, therefore, is not the denial of God's existence but its affirmation: the existence of a God of moral law in whose world what we sow we reap.

Moreover, starting with that much of God one cannot stop there. The God of a moral order must be a God who cares about righteousness, and purposes the downfall of evil and the victory of good; and when faith in such a God undergirds a man, something everlastingly true and solid sustains his hope. The world of such a God can never be hopeless.

Such sustenance we surely need today. I am pleading for creative hopefulness now because, while the winning of the war seems within our grasp, the winning of the peace grows every day more dubious. After the last war Lloyd George described the situation as "the broken waters beneath the great falls." Those of us who have lived near Niagara know what that means, and certainly after this terrific cataract there will be broken waters indeed beneath the falls, whose turmoil no easy-going optimism can possibly survive. The situation we are running into calls for people in whom trouble produces endurance, and endurance character, and character hope, and the question is, Are we going to have enough of them?

Some scenes in history haunt one's imagination. For years the cry rose in Rome, "Carthage must be destroyed," until at last Carthage was destroyed. Scipio the younger won the war and razed Carthage to the ground. Polybius was with him that day in north Africa, and he records that Scipio grasped his hands and said, "A glorious moment, Polybius; but I have a foreboding that some day the same doom will be pronounced on my own country." Five centuries later Saint Jerome, in a litttle monastery in Bethlehem, wrote this to his friend: "The Roman world is falling. . . . The city which has taken the whole world captive is itself taken. . . . Who could believe it; who could believe that Rome, built up through the ages by the conquest of the world, has fallen; that the mother of nations has become their tomb?" So across the centuries move the victories of war, as though the victims always infected the victors with the fatal germs of their own disease; and there can be no end to that tragic process until in a world organized for co-operation the Prince of Peace shall have won his victory.

Well, I refuse to give up hope. I notice this, at least, that every man keeps his hope longest in the realms where he knows most. I talk with physicians; they may be hopeless about everything else, but not about scientific medicine; they know that has a future. I talk with musicians; they may be hopeless about everything besides, but not about music; there is something deep in the heart of man, they say, that will forevermore come back to that. And I talk with those who know most about international affairs, like Dr. Hambro, former president of the League of Nations, and now president of the Norwegian Parliament; he knows all the awful facts and towering problems, but he is not without hope. Paul is right! Hope is not the superficial by-product of favorable circumstances; it springs from a man's character, from what he is, and cares about, and believes in, and underneath all else from his deep conviction that God is not dead, and has not spoken his last word on any subject. Give us enough men and women of such character, and nothing is impossible.

All of us today live a good deal of our time in China. Who can be grateful enough for such characters as Generalissimo and Madame Chiang Kai-shek? Yet only a few years ago the idea that the destiny of China would thus rest in Christian hands would have been a mad dream. When Robert Morrison, the pioneer missionary, started for China, someone asked him incredulously whether he really expected to make any impression on that huge country. "No!" he answered. "No! but I expect *God will*." Well, God has. Give God enough men and women like Morrison, and God could do anything!

"While there is life there is hope," runs the old saying, but a deeper truth emerges when that saying is reversed: "While there is hope there is life." It makes a profound difference, however, by what route one arrives at that indispensable quality of courageous confidence. Alike in personal and public affairs the most resounding triumphs ever won on earth have been won by those in whom, by God's grace, trouble produced endurance, and endurance character, and character hope.

On Believing in Miracles

T HESE are days when life can grow very dull and drab. The world is a sad mess, and any way one looks at it the future is ominous. In dark situations like this our pre-scientific forefathers had at least one ground of hope: they believed in miracles; they thought the incredible might happen any day; as in *Green Pastures*, God could "r'ar back an' pass a miracle." Thus in desperate circumstances, personal or public, that door of hope stood open to the generations that believed in the miraculous.

We modern Christians have almost altogether lost that reliance. Science has revealed the law-abiding processes of both physical and human nature. Cause and consequence joined in an inevitable succession that man cannot break and that God does not break—that idea is firmly in our minds, the working basis of everything we think and do when we are intelligent about it. If by miracle one means the rupture or suspension of nature's law-abiding processes, then miracles are out. Even fundamentalists, who assert their belief in the miraculous, simply believe in miracles that happened some two thousand years ago. They may insist that once an ax-head, lost in a river, floated, that once our Lord walked on the water and raised from the dead a man four days in the tomb, but no more than the rest of us do they practically count on anything like that happening now. If one of our sailors, sunk at sea, should claim that he had been swallowed by a whale and after three days returned safe to land, the fundamentalists would be as incredulous as anyone. So, faith in miracle as a vital, practical affair of day-by-day reliance now, has for most of us disappeared.

Moreover, there is no use trying to get it back again in its

[124]

pre-scientific form, but we may well try to recover some of the hope and confidence, the expectation of the unpredictable, that went along with it. We deeply need to believe that the incredible may happen. Men are saying that it will take a miracle if out of this war we get a peace just and durable enough to forestall another one. Of course it will! The recovery of faith that the miraculous in that sense can happen is one of our profoundest needs.

When a vine has long twined about a trellis, and the trellis, now grown old, rots away, the vine faces a difficult transition period while adjusting itself to a new trellis. The old pre-scientific idea of miracle was a trellis for hope, and now for most of us it has gone, and in consequence the expectation that God can and will do something startling, marvelous, unpredictable, has withered. This morning we are not trying to resurrect the old trellis, but we are trying to re-establish the old hope.

Note to start with that in this endeavor the Christian believer, far from finding science his enemy, as many suppose, finds in science his most illustrious example. The one place in our modern world where belief most holds its ground that the impossible may turn out to be true and the incredible a fact, is science. A hundred and twenty-five years ago 50 per cent of us here would have been pock-marked by smallpox. Today none of us is. In all the annals of the ancient world recording miracles of healing—this individual and that mysteriously recovered from illness by the grace of God—there is nothing to compare with such salvation of whole populations from a plague. Even a century ago it would have been barely credible. So we face the paradox that the essential meaning of "miracle"—indeed, the original meaning of the words for it in the Bible, namely, the marvelous and amazing —has now migrated from the realm of religion to the realm of science.

This is why, say as we will that the old belief in miracle has gone, the word "miracle" persists. We cannot get rid of it. It stands for something real. Life in our modern world is not reduced to the tame level of the ordinary. Never in history did the most intelligent people believe as they do now that the impossible is going to happen and the incredible turn out true. Friends of mine tell me of things going on in scientific laboratories that seem downright unbelievable. The preachers may have ceased talking about miracles, but the scientists have just begun.

The reason for this is clear. When first the idea of the reign of law came in, religious people were thoroughly scared. They thought of law as a prison house, cause and consequence, inexorably joined, shutting them up in close confinement, with no room left for human freedom or Divine providence. If the reign of law was established, they thought, then man's initiative and God's control of human destiny were done for.

Far from being a prison house, however, the knowledge of law-abiding processes has turned out to be one of the most liberating ideas that man ever had. Every time we learn a new law, we can do a new thing. If we can get at the laws of physical nature, then we can handle physical nature and work by means of it miracles our forefathers never dreamed. If we can learn a new law in the realm of psychology, we can achieve new results, curing mental diseases that our fathers in despair ascribed to demons, and opening doors of hope where no hope had ever been. Miracle does not have to mean broken law; the great miracles are wrought not by breaking law but by using law-abiding processes to ends hitherto unbelievable.

If man can thus use law-abiding processes to unexpected and amazing ends, why cannot God do the same? For one who believes in God at all it is absurd to picture him tied hand and foot by laws he has himself ordained. Are not the law-abiding processes of this universe at his disposal at least as much as they are at ours? So the idea of miracle that lately

migrated from the realm of religion to the realm of science
can now migrate back again. When Cowper wrote his hymn,

> God moves in a mysterious way
> His wonders to perform,

he may have thought of God as suspending or breaking natural
law; but now when we think of God as using his own law-
abiding processes to do in and for us things at first incredible,
that hymn is just as true as ever. God does move in a mysterious way, his wonders to perform.

Take a single example from the Bible to illustrate what we
are driving at—the release of those enslaved Hebrews from
Egypt and their launching on an utterly unimaginable career
as one of the world's great peoples. The miraculous legend is
that at the command of Moses a strong east wind drove back
the sea and that the children of Israel walked across dry-shod,
with the waters banked on either side. That is where the modern mind has its difficulty—it cannot believe the legend. But
behind the legend is the fact—the northern extensions of the
Red Sea are sometimes driven dry by a strong east wind, and
only a few years ago Major-General Tulloch saw the Lake
Menzala, a short distance north of the spot where the Hebrews
are supposed to have crossed, driven back seven miles by the
wind, leaving the lake bottom dry. So, we say, *that* is probably
what occurred! But back of both the legend and the probable
fact is the real miracle: an enslaved people, whipped and
beaten, did escape from Egypt—there is no doubt of that—
and as was said of Napoleon, that he made his generals out of
mud, God made one of the most creative peoples in history
out of despised material, concerning which no one could
possibly have foreseen, or in advance believed, the consequence.
Such are the honest-to-goodness miracles of history, beyond
man's expectancy or his power to achieve. So, with no fooling about it,

[127]

> God moves in a mysterious way
>   His wonders to perform;
> He plants his foot-steps in the sea,
>   And rides upon the storm.

As we apply this to ourselves, consider first how deeply we need this point of view if God is to mean anything real to us. Most people today believe in God after a fashion; they are not atheists; they think somebody must have created the universe and started everything going. But a living God whose sovereignty rules over life, whose providence controls life, who is actively working out his purposes in life, and on whom we can rely, if we fulfill his conditions, to do for us in personal and public experience wonders that in advance seem utterly incredible—that real God all too few people possess.

Alas, how many moderns in this desperate generation have no reliance for themselves and for the world save man's power alone to control the law-abiding processes of this universe!

Or is that all that men rely upon? One reason for this sermon is my concern about the prevalent, popular superstitious substitutes for an intelligent faith in the overruling providence of God. We say that in this educated generation men have given up belief in miracles, to believe in scientific law. Upon the contrary, millions have given up an intelligent, ethical, spiritually-minded reliance on God's providence and grace, to believe in astrology, palmistry, numerology, in mediums and fortunetellers, in the power of amulets and endless forms of cheap and superstitious magic. The woods are full of it, as though men instinctively knew that there is something miraculous in the cosmos—

> . . . more things in heaven and earth, Horatio,
>   Than are dreamt of in your philosophy—

and when men do not have an intelligent and expectant faith in God's overruling providence, they find crazy substitutes for it.

Indeed, the situation is worse than that. A Swedish journalist, only lately out of Berlin, has just reported what is going on inside Germany. Again and again he repeats Adolf Hitler's favorite slogan: "To make the impossible possible." So, Hitler believes in that! He nearly made good on that. He did almost achieve the impossible. Our forefathers used to believe not only in Divine miracles but in devils' miracles also —incredible things wrought by evil powers. Well, the only answer to men who believe that in the cause of evil the impossible can be done is men who believe in the name of God that the incredible good can come true and the unpredictable happen.

What we are trying to say, therefore, is desperately needed now. Over against the cheap forms of credulous belief in magic and the terrible forms of evil's belief in its miraculous powers, I believe in the living God, who has never said his last word on any subject or landed his last hammer blow on any task, and in whose world the one thing most certain is that the unbelievable will happen. Throughout history he has been doing the incredible. He did bring an enslaved tribe out of Egypt and make a great people of them. In dire disasters when there seemed no hope, as in the Exile, he did raise up prophets who beyond the possibility of man's foreseeing made of catastrophe the most spiritually productive eras in Israel's life. He did send Christ, turn B.C. into A.D., and make of a man hung on a cross a power stronger and more enduring than Caesar's empire. He has always been doing incredible things that no one could possibly foresee.

Imagine yourself back some millions of years ago on this planet, facing two facts here. On the one side volcanoes— huge, terrific, blazing with the inexhaustible fires of the earth's flaming core, and on the other side protoplasm—microscopic, invisible along the water's edge, feeble, quiet, vital. On which are we betting as we stand there millions of years ago— volcanoes or protoplasm? Protoplasm had no credible chance to mean anything as against the violent forces represented by volcanoes, and yet see what actually came of it at last—life, spirit, beauty, music, prophets, apostles, martyrs, scientists, and saints. The unimaginable did happen. Unpredictability is the essential quality of this cosmos, and in the future as in the past the one thing we can be most sure about is that what will happen will be, as Paul said, what "eye hath not seen, nor ear heard," and that hath not "entered into the heart of man."

Now, that quality of unpredictability belongs not to matter but to spirit. Even when animal life first appears out of the inorganic, unpredictability comes with it. As one scientist put it, "One may take three observations of a comet and three of a cat, but it is safer to predict the date of the comet's return than to tell how the cat will jump." Always a merely material thing—a comet, a volcano—is, on the whole, predictable, but when life and spirit come you cannot tell what may happen. When spirit comes we might get the "Sistine Madonna," or *Hamlet*, or the *Concerto in D Major*, or Einstein's mathematics, or the Sermon on the Mount, or Christ on the cross forgiving his enemies. One never can tell what may happen when spirit comes, for that is always doing the unforeseeable. Such is the quality of this cosmos, and that is what we might expect, if there is a God.

Let us not go on living in a dull, drab world! Even this ghastly era need not get us down! This is still a miraculous universe. In the film *Madame Curie* you recall that when the first faint intimation came of a mysterious power that could take photographs in the dark, Pierre Curie exclaimed, "It would be incredible!" Of course it would be incredible, but it was true! That is the kind of universe we live in—more dimensions to it than our three-dimensional minds can guess, more things in it and ahead of it than are dreamed of in our philosophy.

Today men say that war can never be stopped, that it has always been here, that it is inherent in human nature, that it is an incurable disease. That is exactly what men said with equal truth about chattel slavery—that it had always been here, that it was inherent in human nature, that it was an incurable disease. Believe it or not, the New York *Gazette* for September 4, 1738, carried an advertisement offering for sale: "Englishmen, Cheshire cheese, Negro men, a Negro girl, and a few Welshmen." Only two hundred years ago in this city chattel slavery seemed a disease that only a miracle could cure. Well, such miracles can happen. They always have been happening. And in these days when men like Hitler, believing the impossible possible, undertake incredible things, it would be a pity if we who believe in the living God should not at least match them with an equal faith in the possibilities of a world organized for peace.

Our thought would not be complete, however, if we did not follow it inside our private personal lives to see how deeply we need it there. In one of our most popular musical comedies a very frail and susceptible young woman, explaining why it is that she always gives in to temptation, sings, to the amusement of the audience, "How Can I Be What I Ain't?" At that point I confess I almost forgot to laugh, seeing in imagination a long procession of people whom I have met in personal consultations, with that cry sometimes desperately rising in them: "How Can I Be What I Ain't?" And while a musical comedy is not supposed to be the place for a preacher to get his themes, I fell to thinking that, after all, the central message of the Christian gospel is precisely its answer to that question. When Paul said, "The good which I would I do not: but the evil which I would not, that I practice. . . . Wretched man that I am," he was saying, "How Can I Be What I Ain't?" And when he cried, "I thank God through Jesus Christ our Lord," he was bearing witness to the amazing transformations that the grace and power of God can work in human lives.

Well, why not? If a blazing desert in Arizona, hearing of nature's loveliness, of orange groves and eucalyptus trees, should cry, "How Can I Be What I Ain't?" science would answer, We can change you until even a desert becomes a garden. Science thus walks into life, crying, We can transform things, make them over, until slender filaments that seemed of no account shine with electric light, and substances our fathers never heard of become the indispensable reliance of the modern world! So too a vital religion speaks. No religion is vital until it so speaks, saying: No man need stay the way he is; he can be transformed by the renewing of his mind.

I wish this message could come home now to someone here who needs it. Life does grow dull and drab. We do get sunk in habits that enslave us, discouragements that depress us, evil ways that ruin us. We do need to believe in miracles, the kind of miracle that made Simon the vacillating into Peter the rock, Saul of Tarsus into Paul the Apostle, Augustine the debauchee into Saint Augustine, and that across the centuries has taken innumerable human deserts and made orange groves grow in them. That can happen! That has always been happening! That could happen here today!

In one of the most revealing verses in the Gospels we read that Jesus could do no "mighty works there because of their unbelief." That was the trouble. They had lost faith in the possibility of transforming events in their lives. They had let life iron them out flat, reduce them to an unexpectant dead level, with no hope of inner change. They had forgotten the great truth that when a man is changed inside, then everything is changed for him—his very sins changed, as a disease, long regarded as incurable is shifted now to the list of the curable; his troubles changed because he who handles them has a changed mind. When a man is himself changed, he moves into a changed world. That inner miracle of personal transformation is possible.

Indeed, here is a strange paradox. The common impression is that it is the little, belated, unintelligent minds that believe in miracle; but the fact is that it is the great minds who most believe in unforeseen and incredible possibilities. It is the Luther Burbanks who believe what can be done with thorny cactus. It is the Wilfred Grenfells who believe what can be done in Labrador. It is Christ who believed incredibly in Peter and James and John. Everyone knows Tschaikowsky's *Andante Cantabile*. It is one of the loveliest of his compositions and it will never die. On a summer vacation Tschaikowsky heard a Russian baker singing to himself a popular song which began, "Vanya sat on the divan and smoked a pipe of tobacco." That was what Tschaikowsky started with! That was what he saw the possibilities in and miraculously transformed into the *Andante Cantabile*.

Christ so sees possible miracles in us today, miracles of courage and character, of evil habit overcome and of discouragements surmounted, of health restored through the healing of the mind, of doors closed on an old past and opened on a new future. If you cannot believe it, say this to yourself: He believes it; he always believed it; that is how he got all his Andante Cantabiles—miracles of transformation performed on unlikely material. God grant that today the old verse may not be true of us: "He did not many mighty works there because of their unbelief."

Loyalty, the Basic Condition of Liberty

THE desire to be free, to have the chance to be ourselves, express ourselves, and do as we please, is one of the deepest passions in human nature. We see it in a little child resenting restraint, and we feel it vicariously in whole nations whose liberty has been wrenched from them. It is an appalling thing not to be free. So, the basic struggles of human life can be interpreted as endeavors after emancipation.

Here is a home economically imprisoned, no financial elbow-room, the natural desires of family life confronting every-where the prohibitions of penury. And then affluence comes. What emancipation comes with it: freedom of action, elation of spirit, as though a liberator said, The world belongs to you now—all things are yours!

Or here is a youth reared in a cramped, prohibitive ethic of codes and rules. From his childhood up his community, his church and home have said "Don't" to him, and now, breaking away, he snaps the bondage of old codes and on his own goes out to be himself and express himself. What eman-cipation is there, as though a liberator cried, The whole world now lies before you—all things are yours!

Or here is a nation humiliated and enslaved, with alien gestapos in control and all the freedoms gone. And then re-lease comes, and that instinctive Patrick Henry who is in all men, "Give me liberty, or give me death," has his desires ful-filled, and, master again in its own household the nation cries, All things are ours!

Everywhere in personal and social life the elemental strug-gles of human nature can be interpreted as endeavors after freedom. Yet something is the matter in all this—there is a catch here somewhere. Multitudes of families gain the liberty of affluence and make misery out of it; many youths gain the freedom of self-expression and wreck themselves on it; nations aplenty have won their sovereign statehood and have found neither happiness within nor peace without. "Give me liberty, or give me death," yes! But why do we so often get both? We win liberty and then work our own death by means of it.

Is not this the gist of the matter: liberty was born a twin; liberty and loyalty—they were born together. Liberty, to be free from something; loyalty, to be mastered by something—alas for man or nation that tries to get one without the other!

Consider a saying of Paul that begins with the very phrase we have been using to describe the natural feeling of emancipation: "All things are yours." Paul said that. He was a preacher of freedom. Wherever his gospel went, emancipation came with it, from old codes, old rituals, old racial discriminations. The whole world belongs to you, he wrote to the Corinthians: "All things are yours; whether Paul, or Apollos, or Cephas, or the world, or life, or death, or things present, or things to come." But the rest of that text inseparably goes with it: "All are yours; and ye are Christ's; and Christ is God's." So what belongs to us is matched by what we belong to. Our trouble is that we habitually try to get the first half of that text without the second. What belongs to us—we struggle for that; what we belong to—we forget that. Liberty—that seems infinitely desirable; loyalty—that seems very demanding. Cannot we get one without the other? Cannot we rip that text in two and take but half of it? To have life say to us, All things are yours—that would be joyous. But to have life say, And ye are Christ's—that is serious.

Nevertheless, everywhere one looks at human life the principle of this text holds true. The scientists, for example, want liberty. If anyone demands it, they do—freedom from all coercion and restraint to think with emancipated minds. Yes, but not liberty without loyalty. Recall how Carlyle put it:

"Truth! . . . though the Heavens crush me for following her: no Falsehood! though a whole celestial Lubberland were the price of Apostasy." So, every scientific research laboratory says to the scientist, All things are yours; and ye are truth's.

Today the personal and social agony of the world comes in how large measure from the neglect of this basic principle! Let us watch it at work in one realm after another.

Certainly we face it in our personal ethical living. We all resent moral restraint. Why should these ethical conventionalities, these codes and rules, pen up and contradict our strong desires, and with their prohibitions say "Don't" to our free self-expressions? We will not have it so. We will knock the bungs from our barrels and let our emotions gurgle. We will have liberty and do as we please. That side of the matter has, to a degree unknown before in our lifetime, dominated the moral living of this nation in recent years. But every personal counselor confronts, day after day, the sorry results of this one-sidedness—liberty without loyalty.

In some people liberty without loyalty peters out because, acting as though they were isolated individuals who can do as they please, they find that really they are socially related persons who, doing what they please, cruelly hurt someone else. Then, despite their ethical modernism, conscience steps in, and some emancipated deed that in a moment of ambition or passion they pleased to do moves inexorably from happy anticipation, through committal, into memory, and never looks happy again. They had their liberty, but now like Lady Macbeth they are

>   . . . troubled with thick-coming fancies,
> That keep her from her rest.

With others this one-sidedness of liberty alone peters out because they discover that if they do as they please often enough, repeating it again and again, the time comes when they have to keep on repeating it whether they please or not.

Starting out with liberty, they end in that most unbreakable slavery of habit, forced upon them by their own psychological constitutions. As another put it: "There are only two stages in the life of the drinker: (1) when he could stop if he would, and (2) when he would stop if he could."

Clearly, then, there is something the matter with ethical liberty alone, not because of artificial moral codes but because of our essential social relatedness and our own psychological make-up. We are so made that liberty without loyalty ruins us. So one young woman who had lived an emancipated life committed suicide and wrote in explanation: "I am killing myself because I have never sincerely loved any human being all my life." Alas what thin fodder, in the end, liberty without loyalty turns out to be!

This is the nub of the matter, is it not: liberty alone is not an organizing principle; it puts nothing together; it is dispersive. Within society it produces autonomous, irresponsible individuals, confusedly following their private whims, and within the individual it sets our various emotions and desires going every which way, doing as they please. Liberty alone is not an organizing principle—it does not draw us together into one-directional, purposeful, integrated living; but loyalty does. "All things are yours"—that by itself alone scatters us. "And ye are Christ's"—that unifies us.

This was Paul's special problem. He probably broke through as many moral and ritual prohibitions as any man in history ever did in one lifetime. Of how many old restrictions he cried, "Where the Spirit of the Lord is, there is liberty," "For freedom did Christ set us free"! But if he had stopped there, he would not have been Paul. What made him Paul was that his liberty was founded upon loyalty: All things are mine—he was a freeman; and I am Christ's—he was a devotee.

Michelangelo wanted to be free. He had a foolish family who tried to repress and prohibit him. They wanted him to be a moneymaker. When he so much as spoke of art they beat him to enforce submission. He desperately craved freedom, and at last manfully struck out for it, broke away from his imprisoning home and denied its claims upon him. He was a real person, but mark what made him that! As he walked out that famous day into freedom, he was saying, Now all the world belongs to me; and I belong to beauty and to art.

To some youth here this message might well come. You want to do as you please. Of course you do! As a minister of Christ I crave that for you. It is a great privilege. But long ago Saint Augustine laid down the basic condition on which alone that kind of life can successfully be lived: "Love God, and do as you please." That is Christianity at its very center. Love God; give your freely chosen inner loyalty to the Highest; belong in your secret personal devotion to the Christ, as a real scientist belongs to truth or a real artist to beauty, and then, being that kind and quality of person, do as you please!

Consider now that this principle applies just as much to our democracy as a whole as it does to our personal moral living. We may not blame the plight of the democracies today simply on the attack of the dictatorships. Democracy would not be in this sorry case if it had not fallen sick, and it has fallen sick of this very disease of which we speak. It has come to mean to multitudes, rights and not duties, liberty but not loyalty, what they can get out of the country not what they can give to it. Then the dictatorships arise, saying to their citizens, You belong to the state; your life's highest meaning is to live and die for the state. Thus the world splits up, dictatorship naturally emphasizing loyalty but not liberty, democracy naturally emphasizing liberty but not loyalty. Somehow we must get those two indispensable qualities together.

How commonly our democracy in America has pictured itself in our imaginations as though from an affluent cornucopia it poured out its opportunities and privileges before us! All things are yours, it says. Dictatorship cries, You must! But democracy says, You may—you may think, speak, print, do, enjoy, in freedom of life and enterprise.

From these terrific days we are living through now we ought to learn something. For this disaster teaches clearly that we cannot maintain our democracy by interpreting it mainly as the right to do as we please. Here too liberty, taken by itself alone, creates a multitude of irresponsible individuals, each living as he pleases for what he can get out of it, and as well classes of individuals, pressure groups, and selfish economic interests, whether of capital or labor, organized not for what they can contribute to the nation but for what they can obtain from it. Liberty alone stresses only one word out of three: "independence"—my personal independence, my group's independence. But there are two other words: "interdependence"—for the very essence of democracy is co-operation; and "dependence"—dependence on the whole world's communal life and on the laws of God that underlie it. The claim of independence without the recognition of interdependence and dependence is one of the greatest delusions in the world; it is liberty without loyalty, and that is one of democracy's major temptations.

Democracy naturally does emphasize privilege and right, and we who are democracy's children have it to thank for priceless gifts of open doors and free opportunities. But such a story of privilege, right, and opportunity is only half of democracy, and that half was not the one which created it in the first place. It took loyalty to create it. Remember what John Adams, the founding father, wrote in a letter: "Posterity! you will never know how much it cost the present generation to preserve your freedom! I hope you will make a good use of it. If you do not, I shall repent it in heaven that I ever took half the pains to preserve it."

The result of this truth is serious, and it strikes at every one of us. Said one American the other day, "What we need is the drill sergeant in American life; we want to get some discipline into our young people." You know why he said that. He sees democracy interpreted as rights and not duties becoming rampant, irresponsible individualism, and he reaches out for the first handy thing to stop it—the drill sergeant idea. But that is hitlerism; it is dictatorship's solution. If we do not want that solution in business, in journalism, in education, in personal life, the alternative is plain: liberty, founded on voluntary loyalty to the common good. That, the price of democracy's origin, is the price of its maintenance as well: freely given loyalty to justice, fair play, brotherhood, care for the welfare of all, especially for the lowliest and the least. Either we will achieve that or we will get the drill sergeant. At that point Christianity and democracy preach the same gospel: All things are yours—freedom, privilege, right, opportunity; and ye are Christ's.

Turn now to see this principle lighted up when it is illustrated in the realm of religion itself, for religious freedom is one of the major tenets of our faith, and nowhere is liberty more commonly interpreted in negative terms. We are not compelled to be Methodists or Baptists, Presbyterians or Episcopalians, Protestants or Catholics; we are free. We do not have to subscribe to any creed as the condition of citizenship, as once was true in Massachusetts, for example; we are free. Freedom of worship—what a boon it is and how incredible it once seemed to our forefathers who lacked it! If only, they prayed, we could have liberty to worship God according to the dictates of our own consciences! And now freedom of worship is the possession of millions of Americans—who never worship. Talk to them about religious liberty and they say they would die for it. All things are ours, they say; we are free from all restrictions in religion. But the rest of the text is dropped out—religious liberty without religious loyalty.

This is particularly the problem of liberal Protestantism. We have fought a great fight for liberty. We have said about innumerable ancient superstitions and incredibilities, You do not have to believe all that to be a Christian; you are free. And multitudes have followed us, rejoicing that they were relieved from the intolerable burden of such old incumbrances. Every liberal Protestant preacher says to his people, All things are yours: all modern science, the best philosophy, the light that falls on life from any source—all are yours. And this message of emancipation has been welcomed, as gospels of liberty always are. But today as one listens to the most serious minds in the church one catches another note with a deeper accent in it, as though to say, To be free from old incredibilities is not enough—that is hardly half a gospel; we will not surrender that half, but today the world desperately needs the other half, too: ye are Christ's. Negative liberty without such positive loyalty is no religion at all. It is the latter half of that text that goes to the heart of the matter. We belong to someone. A man living in this cosmos as though there were nothing here greater than he is, on which he depends, and to which his fidelity rightfully belongs, is not fully a man.

> Make me a captive, Lord,
> And then I shall be free;
> Force me to render up my sword,
> And I shall conq'ror be.

How many of us are taking that in earnest?

Was there ever a time in human history when it was more plain that what belongs to us can never save us, and that what we belong to is the crux of the matter? Never before have so many voices said to mankind, All things are yours. Notably that is the message of applied science. See the mastery it gives us over the latent and exhaustless resources of the cosmos! In my own lifetime I have seen electric locomotion come, and the telephone, the radio, the automobile, the airplane. Look ahead a thousand years—are not all things ours? Well, are they, if we go on like this? And the decisive element in the situation is not what more things can belong to us, but what high things we belong to.

Mankind does need science; but science without religion —that is, mastery over things without being mastered by supreme spiritual devotions—is the definition of hell on earth. This world catastrophe is not an argument against Christianity but a plea for it. Until we belong personally and socially to Christ and what he stands for, nothing that belongs to us will benefit us much. As for us who are religious liberals, "For freedom did Christ set us free." Paul too rejoiced in that but he went further: "Paul," so he began his letter to the Romans, "a bondservant of Jesus Christ."

Finally, from these more extended illustrations of our truth come home to our own personal emotional lives. Such a plea for loyal self-commitment to Christ and what he stands for as we are making sounds to some, dour, demanding; it costs sacrifice, they think; it means giving up things they want to do, and disciplining life in subjection to an inner fidelity. They dislike the prospect. They want freedom in its loose and natural sense—that is joy, they say. But we had better face the fact that it is not joy. Looseness of life is not happiness. "The man without a country," the man with nothing he is devoted to and lives for, has never been a symbol of anything but wretchedness. It is our loyalties that make life emotionally worth living.

What have been the great hours of our lives, rememberable to our dying day? They are the hours when we were carried out of ourselves by something that mastered us—the breathtaking sweep of great mountains, the spell of great music, inner dedication to a cause concerning which we said, Not my will, thine be done, or the love of some person to whom we pledged deathless fidelity, "to have and to hold from this day forward, for better for worse, for richer for poorer, in sickness and in health, to love and to cherish, till death us do part." It is our loyalties that make life worth living.

A mother has a child. She belongs to the child. She is not free. Day and night that child rules her with a thralldom stronger than a rod of iron. Then the child dies. Now she is free; she can come and go as she will; no voice calling her now makes her run at its bidding. But see this strange woman heartbroken at her new-found freedom! This liberty of hers is the heaviest burden ever laid upon her. If we could give her back her child, if the old sense of belonging could return again, then she would feel free and be herself once more. We human beings are much more complex than we take ourselves for. We think we want liberty, but the only liberty worth having is founded on loyalty.

Here is the strange paradox of all rich and fulfilled living. We do want to be free from external restraints, from moral and political dictators and tyrants, but when we ask why we want to be free, we run straight into a paradoxical answer: We crave liberty so that we may find loyalty, may freely give ourselves to something that masters us, saying to it, I belong to you; you shall organize my life, shall save me from aimlessness and give direction and meaning to my days.

So, wanting to be mastered now, finding life vain, futile, aimless unless it is given to something, we seek our supreme loyalty. But when we ask why we want thus to be loyal, we face the paradox again. We want to be mastered so that we can be free, so that whatever is best in us can flower out, emancipated and fulfilled, life saved from anarchy to integration, from aimlessness to purposefulness and meaning.

This strange paradox, that we want freedom in order to choose our loyalty, and want loyalty in order to be free, is true of every one of us, for here is the very definition of freedom: Liberty is the substitution of inner voluntary loyalty for outward constraint.

The other day I saw a man who had lived an emancipated

life—loose, irresponsible, unorganized, aimless, futile—a sorry mess of misery he had ended in. Then I went home and read again the story of Andrew Melville, one of the early Scotch reformers, threatened, one day, by the Earl of Morton with death by hanging if he did not cease his free speaking. And Melville laughed. "Tush, sir," he said, in words that every Scot remembers, "threaten your courtiers after that manner. It is the same to me whether I rot in the air or in the ground. It will not be in your power to hang or exile his truth."

Which of these two, this loose, undedicated fellow, or Andrew Melville, was really free? And which of these two does the world need today? Ah, church of Christ, at any rate, keep your message clear: Liberty, all things are yours, founded on loyalty, ye are Christ's, and Christ is God's.

A Time To Stress Unity

IN THE first chapter of John's Gospel we read: "Philip findeth Nathanael, and saith unto him, We have found him, of whom Moses in the law, and the prophets, wrote, Jesus of Nazareth, the son of Joseph. And Nathanael said unto him, Can any good thing come out of Nazareth?" Nathanael had a prejudice against all Nazarenes. Gathering up in his dislike an entire group of people, he would believe no decent thing about any of them. One wonders how he reached that state of mind. Had some Nazarene once cheated him or treated him discourteously, and had he generalized his resentment until it became inclusive contempt for the whole group? Or had Nazareth in general made itself unpopular so that ugly rumors ran about the countryside, believing which, Nathanael hated the entire town? There Nathanael stands, at any rate, a classic example of the kind of prejudice that curses the world today. No longer thinking of the men, women, and children of Nazareth as persons, one by one, he gathered up in his dislike the whole group, tagged them with one label, and despised them all.

Thereby he nearly missed the Christ. "Jesus of Nazareth," said Philip. That was enough for Nathanael: "Can any good thing come out of Nazareth?"

Contemporary parallels to that kind of prejudice are plentiful. Multitudes harbor it without recognizing either the public menace involved in it or its implicit denial of every basic Christian idea of God and man. Nathanael himself, guilty of one of the most destructive sins on earth, probably never thought of it as sin at all. He despised Nazarenes. Well, cannot a man have his likes and dislikes? Why should he not harbor an inclusive prejudice against all Nazarenes if he feels like it?

Many kinds of evil are clearly recognized as such—brutal, sensual, criminal—but here is a sin, subtle, quiet, decently clothed and commonly found in respectable places, that none-theless is one of the most ruinous menaces on earth. Nathanael was far from being a bad man. When Jesus first saw him he called him "an Israelite . . . in whom is no guile!" A highly respectable person Nathanael was, but he was guilty of a kind of sin that Archbishop Spellman of our own city has rightly called a cancerous growth. It is a dreadful thing to be Nathanael—moving in the best circles, eminently respectable, sitting even in the pews of a church like this, yet guilty of one of man's most damnable and destructive evils: an in-clusive prejudice against a whole human group.

One of the ironies of our day is that Hitler should proclaim what he calls a new world order while all the time the basic ideas of that new order are taken from primitive barbaric times, and among them nothing more dastardly than his edition of Nathanael's sin—anti-Semitism. Centuries before Christ Aristotle said, "Greeks owe no more duties to the bar-barians than to the wild beasts." Aristotle was a good man, but still he was guilty of a sin whose consequence is one of his-tory's chief horrors. And now naziism is giving us an example of what that sin of Nathanael and of Aristotle, and of many Americans too, means when it is full grown—some two million Jews brutally tortured and slain in Europe.

Today, then, concerning this sin of group prejudice, whose bitter accents one hears in our clubs and churches and dinner table conversations, what we are really saying is, Don't be a Nazi! One of the noblest utterances of this war was a statement made in 1940—desperate days those were in Britain —by Dr. Temple, then Archbishop of York, now Archbishop of Canterbury: "The spirit in which we fight matters more than our winning. If we go Nazi and then win, it will be the same for the world as if the Nazis win. But if we keep charity alive with courage, our victory will be a boon to mankind and our defeat would be a redemptive agony." We Americans need to heed that admonition now, for the growth of certain Nazi elements in America—especially race prejudice—is appalling.

Apply this in the place where for many it is now most difficult, namely, to the Japanese. Roiled with horror, turbulent with indignation, we have heard of the beastly cruelties the Japanese military have perpetrated on British and American prisoners. Nowhere has the essential brutality of war been more terribly exhibited. Our moral indignation is justified, but for all that, beware of Nathanael's sin: do not become a Nazi! We should be profoundly grateful for men like Joseph C. Grew, our former Ambassador to Japan! He knows the Japanese, if any American does. He never lumps them in one group—an insane way of thinking; he never tags them with one label—a sure sign that intelligence has surrendered to passion. Even when in Japan he saw the worst rising to the top, ruthlessly preparing to plunge the whole Pacific world into disaster, and he wrote, "For me there are no finer people in the world than the best type of Japanese"; and for our American-born Japanese he pleads now: "Like the Americans of German descent, the overwhelming majority of Americans of Japanese origin wish to be and are wholly loyal to the United States, and not only that, but they wish to prove that loyalty in service to their native land."

In any situation at any time, no matter what the emotional provocation is, to lump a whole race or nation in an inclusive prejudice and hatred is as ignorant as it is unchristian. Nathanael was a highly respectable person, but that sin of his was dreadful.

Consider further that Nathanael was taking an attitude toward another group that he would not have wanted taken toward his own. What race or nation among us could stand having our evils generalized as characteristic of the whole population, so that we were all estimated in terms of our worst? Let the Golden Rule once get into the center of the picture, and race prejudice is out.

The world's colored races today are prejudiced against the United States. Moreover, they can give you the facts. In the last fifty years five thousand persons have been lynched in this country, a large percentage of them Negroes and many of them under circumstances—tortured, burned alive—that beggar description. That kind of thing is known all over the world, and when some people think of America they think of our treatment of American Negroes, and, contemplating a victory of the white races, they ask, Can any good come out of that? Well, would you think that fair to America?

When we read about the caste system in India, especially about the untouchable class—outlawed, segregated, despised —we think that appalling. Listen, then! Benjamin E. Mays, a Negro gentleman, Doctor of Philosophy, President of Morehouse College, sometime since visited India. Here is what he says:

> The students followed me in crowds—not because I had anything special to say but because I was a Negro from America and the students wanted to know more about the way white Americans treat Negroes and why they deny them the democracy they preach. The most striking incident was my visit to an "untouchable" school for boys. The Master ... literally begged me to visit them, be their guest at meal and address the boys. I accepted the invitation. When he introduced me he made it clear that I was a Christian, from Christian America; yet he emphasized at the same time that I was an "untouchable" in America—"an untouchable like us," he emphasized. I was dazed, puzzled, a bit peeved. It had never occurred to me. But instantly I recognized that there was an element of truth in what he said. As long as Negroes are treated as second and third class citizens, whether in the North where segregation and discrimination are spreading, where Negroes are frequently denied the privileges of eating in restaurants and denied occupancy in

hotels, where discrimination against them in employment and civic life is rampant; or whether in the South, where segregation and discrimination exist by law and where gross inequalities exist in education, politics and work opportunities, they are the "untouchables" of America.

That kind of thing is in the minds of the colored peoples around the world, so that this group prejudice we practice on others is a boomerang.

Would not we Americans wish to say to all the colored peoples on earth: Try to be just to us; we do face a complicated and difficult problem; we brought the Negroes here against their will, long held them as slaves, and now that they are free confront a situation that the wisest of both blacks and whites know is going to take time and patience to work out; North and South alike, the overwhelming mass of our people hate the things you hate, lynching especially. Thank God that is on its way out! In 1941 there were only four lynchings—we are winning that battle.

Would not we Americans wish to say to the colored peoples of the world: We know better than you do our failures in handling this problem of race relationships. In the First World War the first soldier of the American Expeditionary Force in France to get the *Croix de Guerre*, with star and palm, was a Negro sergeant, Henry Johnson; in this war the first American soldier to die after Pearl Harbor was a Negro, Private Robert Brooks. Yet only the other day a young second lieutenant, a Negro, in the uniform of our nation, in one of our great cities, not in the South, was beaten by a policeman merely because he went into a railroad station restaurant for lunch. The great mass of our people, we would say, are humiliated, penitent, ashamed of this disgraceful stormtrooper naziism. But nonetheless, we see reasons for encouragement, too. In Richmond, Virginia, the leading paper of the city has been carrying magnificent editorials pleading for the ending of Jim Crow segregation, and in New York

City recently something happened that gives us hope. A Negro and a white man ran against each other for a judgeship, an important position carrying a salary of $17,000 a year. The Negro won, getting his majority of votes, mark it, in white districts. Then the defeated candidate gave a dinner to his successful Negro rival, and Catholics, Protestants, Jews and Negroes dined together in his honor.

Be just to us, we Americans would wish to say to the world's colored races, and believe the best in us as we try to work this problem out. It is not easy, and God helping us we will do better. Well, wanting and needing such consideration from others, whatsoever we would that men should do unto us, even so let us do unto them! Nathanael, it will not do for you to say, Can any good come out of Nazareth? You could not stand having that said about your own group.

Consider further that Nathanael's group prejudice was not simply a sin against morals, as expressed in the Golden Rule, but a sin against intelligence, too. I shall not trouble you with a learned discussion of the scientific explanation of racial differences except to say that the consensus of modern scientific opinion is summed up in the words of Professor Conklin of Princeton University: "Biology and the Bible agree that 'God hath made of one blood all nations of men.' " This fake science that Hitler so vociferously proclaims, that there are master races and permanently inferior and superior races, has not a leg to stand on. The barbarians, that Aristotle said the Greeks had no more duties toward than toward the wild beasts, were our forefathers; races rise and fall; their diversities—color, aptitudes, and characteristics—are due not to original and permanent differences in their inalienable constitution but to circumstances, geographical conditions, mutations that are alterable and sometimes reversible. Racial prejudice as it is commonly exhibited and sometimes argued for today is thoroughly unintelligent.

Moreover, it is practically, as well as theoretically, unintelligent. Even if Nazareth was as bad as Nathanael thought it was, merely to despise it was not the answer. Something ought to be done about it. For we cannot get rid of Nazareth. There it is, a part of our social environment, its diseases contagious for us and our children, its evils impinging on our households.

People today point to the appalling record of crime among our Negro people. It is appalling. "In 1940," we read, "the Negro crime rate, judged by commitments to prisons and reformatories, was five times that for whites." But the answer to that is neither to deny it nor to meet it with contempt and prejudice. The answer is to do something about it. Here in New York's Harlem in one block 3,871 of our colored people live. If the entire population of the United States were similarly crowded together, all the 135,000,000 of us would be living in one-half the area of greater New York. Of course the crime rate for Negroes is greater than for whites, and it will be until for our own sakes if not for theirs we help them to achieve more decent conditions of living.

Group prejudice is not the answer to anything. It is theoretically unintelligent and practically insane. Nathanael should have read again the Book of Ruth in his own sacred Scriptures. That is all about race prejudice. Can any good come out of Moab, the Jews were saying, and then, so the great story runs, Ruth came out of Moab, she who said to her Jewish mother-in-law, "Entreat me not to leave thee, and to return from following after thee; for whither thou goest, I will go; and where thou lodgest, I will lodge; thy people shall be my people, and thy God my God; where thou diest, will I die, and there will I be buried: the Lord do so to me, and more also, if aught but death part thee and me." Ruth came out of Moab, concerning whom it stands written, she was the mother of Obed, "he is the father of Jesse, the father of David." My soul! Could any good come out of Moab?

As for us Christians, let no one say that today I am talking merely sociology. I am talking Christianity. Race prejudice is as thorough a denial of the Christian God as atheism is and it is a much more common form of apostasy. Race prejudice denies the universal fatherhood of God; it denies the New Testament's insistence on the equality of all souls before God; it denies the central affirmation of the gospel, that God so loved the world that he gave his Son, and as for Jesus of Nazareth, who took his hero, the Good Samaritan, from a despised race, anyone who harbors race prejudice parts company with him.

The climax of our theme, however, brings the whole matter even closer home to these present days. Why could not Nathanael have seen that he was living in a time of discord and division, when the world in general and his own people in particular needed all the unity they could anyhow achieve? He was not helping any by adding to the dissension. We say that this is a generation when races and nations are torn asunder by hatred and violence, but all the more because of that it is a generation when men and women are needed who forget every division that can be forgotten, rise above every difference that can be surmounted, and emphasize every factor that brings men together. This is a time to stress unity.

The Swedish journalist, Arvid Fredborg, recently out of Germany, reports some surprising things going on there, but nothing more surprising than in these sentences: "One must not lay too much emphasis on the differences between Catholicism and Protestantism [in Germany] for in the face of common pressure many barriers have fallen. Catholic priests preach in Protestant churches, and Protestant pastors expelled from their parishes have enjoyed the support of funds which Nazism so far has not been able to rob from the Roman Church." Catholic priests preaching in Protestant pulpits and Protestant pastors living on Catholic funds is strange business, and doubtless it will not outlast the common peril, but it illustrates our theme. A time like this does not simply tear people apart, it also draws them together. The United States and Russia—strange bedfellows! But they illustrate the fact that this is not simply a time of division; it is a time for unity.

This, then, is our sermon. Rise above every prejudice you can surmount, and throw the weight of your influence on all the unity in the nation and in our human race that you can get your eyes upon—folk who do that are the need of the world.

It is a great day in a man's life when, like Nathanael, he is cured of a prejudice. For Nathanael was cured—he became a disciple of Jesus of Nazareth. That kind of transformation is deeply needed now. Group prejudice is a contagious disease; he who harbors it is a public menace; to be cured of it is a public boon. Here are some verses written by an Australian soldier in the South Seas that were picked up by American soldiers and rewritten in their own terms, concerning which you may be sure that they come straight out of personal experience:

Many a mother in America,
When the busy day is done,
Sends a prayer to the Almighty
For the keeping of her son,
Asking that an angel guide him,
And bring him safely back—
Now we see those prayers are
Answered on the Owen Stanley track.

Though they haven't any halos—
Only holes slashed through their ears,
And their faces marked with tattoos
And their hair done up in smears;
Bringing back the badly wounded,
Just as steady as a hearse,
Using leaves to keep the rain off,
And as gentle as a nurse.

[153]

Slow and careful in bad places,
On the awful mountain track
And the look upon their faces
Makes you think that Christ was black.
Not a move to hurt the wounded,
As they treat him like a saint,
It's a picture worth recording,
That an artist's yet to paint.

Many a lad will see his mother,
And husbands see their wives,
Just because the Fuzzy Wuzzys
Carried them to save their lives
From mortar or machine-gun fire,
Or chance surprise attack,
To the care of waiting doctors
At the bottom of the track.

May the mothers of America
When offering a prayer,
Mention these impromptu angels
With the fuzzy-wuzzy hair.*

If one has eyes to see, what good things can come out of
Nazareth!

* So far as available information goes, these verses in their
original form were written by Sapper Bert Beros, a Canadian by
birth and an Australian by adoption.

*Worshiping the Gods of a Beaten Enemy**

O N THIS Sunday after Thanksgiving Day our thoughts
turn naturally to a public theme. Despite the grim
situation that confronts us and the long hard days that
lie ahead, we have much to be grateful for. Nevertheless, who
of us, watching what is going on within our nation now and
foreseeing what awaits us when victory comes, can fail to
feel his thankfulness sobered by profound concern? Today
I share with you what seems to me the basic underlying
reason why that concern is justified. All history teaches at least
one lesson about war—its inevitable tendency to lead the
victor to take on the character of the vanquished. A paradox
it may be but its exhibitions darken history's pages, that in
fighting our enemies we copy them, and in our victories over
them assume ourselves the very attributes and qualities we
have fought against.

Far back in Hebrew history, so the Second Book of Chron-
icles informs us, Judah won a war over the Edomites, and
Amaziah, the Judean king, came back in triumph to Jerusalem.
But then we read, "He brought the gods of the children of
Edom, and set them up to be his gods, and bowed down himself before them, and burned incense unto them." So, he won
a resounding victory and then worshiped the gods of his
beaten enemy. And the Scripture says, "Wherefore the anger
of the Lord was kindled against Amaziah, and he sent unto
him a prophet, who said unto him, Why hast thou sought
after the gods of the people, which have not delivered their
own people out of thy hand?"

If at first sight Amaziah's conduct seems absurd, consider
how easily that ancient scene can be translated into what is

* Preached on November 21, 1943.

[155]

happening now. Is not war itself essentially a process in which we copy our enemies and serve their gods? If they conscript armies, we must conscript armies, too. If they centralize vast powers in a totalitarian government to wage war effectively, we must centralize vast powers in our government as well. If they impose censorship and govern by bureaucracy, our imitation of them is prompt and thorough. If they strip their universities of humane studies and center everything on war, we do the same—"As in Europe," reports one of our American foundations, "so here at home, liberal education has been discarded for the duration. Our universities are now the instrumentalities of total war." If our enemies send their sons to bomb whole cities into desolation and death, we send our sons to do the same, and as they turn their inventive genius and mass their industry to provide new machinery of ruin, so do we. That is war—fighting fire with fire, paying the devil in his own coin. A strange paradox war presents, that, calling other men our enemies and proclaiming that we hate their ways and their ideas, we proceed at once with utmost speed and zeal to imitate them.

Were this fateful process confined to war's conduct only, our problem would be simpler than it is. But, as in Amaziah's case, the temptation to worship the gods of our beaten enemies invades the post-war era. Alexander the Great conquers the Orient, and lo, the Orient conquers Alexander, ruining his simple Grecian court and debilitating his native Grecian valor with Oriental luxury and vice! He too worshiped the gods of his beaten enemies and fell. That tragedy has been too often repeated in history for us to doubt its danger, and he who cannot see that we confront it now is blind indeed. In the end, we shall win this war, we say. Yes, but what if then we worship the gods of our beaten enemies?

In one regard this temptation is obvious, namely, in the drift by which in fighting a totalitarian state we become a totalitarian state ourselves. We say we are fighting naziism and fascism, but in their essential nature what are they? They are the extreme glorification of the state, and the concentration of all power in the state's hands. As Mussolini himself phrased the slogan of fascism: "Everything in the State, nothing against the State, nothing outside the State." So this enemy we fight makes the state, as it were, God, Hitler even saying, "We do not want any other God than Germany itself." Today, then, I am not stepping outside my realm to talk politics, but am talking religion when I stress the fact that here in America now, fighting a centralized totalitarian state that makes itself God, we are dreadfully tempted to become a totalitarian state ourselves, until the governor of Maryland said recently that unless federal bureaucracy is checked it will "do more to destroy the America we love than all the outside enemies that could be ranged against us." It is not often that a Christian minister can quote Nietzsche with approval, but one thing he said is pertinent to our situation now: "When you fight a monster, beware lest you become a monster."

Anyone who makes of this a matter of partisan politics only, supposing that a mere shift of political control will mend it, does not see the problem in its full dimensions. Totalitarianism is not an accident or the mere work of wicked men. It rises naturally out of social turmoil. When everything is chaotic, someone must take charge; a führer of some kind is desperately called for and is popularly welcomed. Then when centralized control has taken charge it is easy to glorify the result.

We say we are fighting the peril of totalitarianism, but with what benign analogies can the totalitarian state be compared! When the symphony orchestra plays, every man there with meticulous obedience follows the conductor's baton. This first violinist does not play as he will; these kettledrums and cymbals are not free to indulge their whims. No musician there talks of individual liberty at all. They are docile, quick to obey, drilled in concerted action under one baton, and, because they are not free, one by one, to play as they will, they are free all together to interpret the compositions of the masters. Such, say the Nazis and Fascists, is the true nature of the state. So Dr. Albert Matthias, not with regret but with pride, said of Germany during the last war: "The government regulates and controls not only the acts but the thoughts of its citizens."

Those of us who come from the old American tradition of liberty and who still believe it, are sure that that analogy is false. A great and free nation is not like a symphony orchestra; that comparison is utterly misleading. To be sure, I am not pleading for what is popularly called "rugged individualism." That is a frontier virtue, and the old frontier conditions are no longer here. Of course, there must be changes in governmental functions; of course, the vast technical advances in our economic life compel extension of political control; to be sure, we have moved into a new era when the old slogan, that government is best which governs least, is nonsense, and we must adjust ourselves to a much more affirmative concept of the state; but to us as Americans and as Christians, the warning of our text is pertinent as centralized power grows ominously among us to totalitarian proportions: Why seek ye after the gods of the people, which have not delivered their own people out of your hands?

Already one hears voices pleading that after this war America be militarized—universal conscription, universal military service and all the rest. But that is the very road down which our enemies walked to reach the result that we now fight against. Universal military service can be presented in beguiling terms, but watch that kitten—it has a way of growing up and turning out to be a tiger!

In the end, if stage by stage it grows to its full stature, it means the manhood and womanhood of the nation mobilized and drilled in docility. It means a vast military establishment, huge munition syndicates, a powerful military caste. It means the increasing federalizing of power, and at last it means the consequence that Mirabeau put into a phrase exactly describing our enemies today: "Not a country with an army but an army with a country." This is one reason why an international society, with sufficient authority and power to insure international security, is now an absolute necessity. It is the only alternative to America's becoming a totalitarian, militarized state. May God save us from that! Were that tragic consequence to happen, it would be Amaziah over again: "He brought the gods of the children of Edom, and set them up to be his gods, and bowed down himself before them."

Consider another side of this matter that may well give us Americans concern. About the most damnable aspect of the Nazi philosophy is its racial prejudice, that on the Jews especially has visited the most barbarous cruelty that even they have suffered since the Middle Ages. This whole idea of a master race, ordained by inherent superiority to rule over other races, seems to us absurd in fact and devilish in consequence—as, for example, when the Nazi leader, Dr. Ley, writes in an article published in 1940, "An inferior race needs less food and less culture than a superior race. Never can the German man live in the same way as the Pole or the Jew."

Yet, deeply as we abhor such insufferable racial pride in nazidom, we Americans need humbly to recognize that not there alone but here as well war is a dreadful roiler of turbulent emotions. Hatred and prejudice thrive everywhere in wartime. Here too scapegoats are sought for popular wrath to vent itself upon; here too anti-Semitism reaches dangerous proportions—interracial tensions are perilous, and racial riots have disgraced our streets. I know that among us all this is not a matter of governmental policy as it is in nazidom. Thank heaven for that! But all the more it is our responsibility as individual citizens to see to it that in fighting Nazis we do not become Nazis. Here in New York we live in a city where there are fourteen foreign language daily newspapers published even in wartime, where there are more people of the German race than there are—or were—in Bremen, more of the Italian race than there are in Florence, more Jews than ever dreamed of living in Jerusalem, and nearly 460,000 Negroes as well. There is no place on earth where racial prejudice, once let it get going, would be so dastardly and so dangerous as in America.

Especially we need to abjure the whole Nazi philosophy of race in dealing with our Negro people—twelve million of them. We, the white race, brought them here against their will, and kept them in slavery until eighty years ago. The responsibility primarily is ours and it cannot be handled on the Nazi basis. We all know the unfair discrimination that makes the Negro people resentful. Of course they are resentful; they ought to be; we would be, too. Here, for example, is the plea of a young Negro student. I see no answer to a plea like this except humbly to acknowledge that it is justified: "If you discriminate against me because I am uncouth, I can become mannerly. If you ostracize me because I am unclean, I can cleanse myself. If you segregate me because I am ignorant, I can become educated. But if you discriminate against me because of my color, I can do nothing. God gave me my color. I have no possible protection against race prejudice but to take refuge in cynicism, bitterness, hatred, and despair."

And now the whole Orient, made up of colored races, is watching us, and one of the best friends Japan has in Asia today is the impression of us that spreads there, strengthened by every evidence of racial prejudice here, as though to say, The Americans fight the Nazis but still they worship the gods of their enemies. Herbert Agar cannot be suspected of being softheaded or super-idealistic. Yet listen to him: "Heretofore the white man has been dominant. Now he discovers that he is outnumbered by the colored races and is himself a minority. He had better quickly decide to join the human race. Soon it will be too late."

This racial question is only one aspect of the larger matter that war inevitably presents—the stirring up of turbulent emotions, the rise of unreasoning prejudice and hate. On that matter the most moving word yet spoken, so it seems to me, has just come from Norway. If ever a people had a right to vengeful prejudice and hatred, it is the Norwegians now. Yet in a statement issued by the Christian leaders of Norway they say: To be sure, war criminals must be punished; justice and the hope of future law and order demand that; but they must be punished by courts of law, after due process and fair trial; there must be no private and personal vindictiveness and vengeance even when the chance comes. And when you ask these Norwegian Christians why, their answer ought to sober and chasten us: "If our people were to give way to their passions we would be starting the new day in Norway by violating God's righteousness. Then the spirit of Naziism would have triumphed over us despite everything, because we would have become what they were." That is the nub of the matter. In fighting the Nazis, God keep us from becoming what they are! Every American needs to face this question: Why seek we after the gods of the people, who have not delivered their own people out of our hands?

The climax of this matter comes when we face the underlying philosophy of our enemies, for we are tempted to imitate not only their political ideas of the state and their emotional glorification of prejudice and hatred, but their undergirding convictions.

When the Nazis started out to do what they have done, they saw clearly that they could not do it on the basis of the Christian faith, and so, under the leadership of men like Rosenberg, they deliberately undertook to displace Christianity—its faith, its institutions, its education of the young, its rituals and celebrations—with a substitute religion based on the old Nordic myths and exalting the old Nordic gods. As Hitler himself said, "We shall wash off the Christian veneer and bring out a religion peculiar to our race."

To be sure, most of us would not become Nazi as explicitly

as that, but who can feel the awful pressures and necessities
of war—the exaltation of brute strength, the reliance on materialistic might, what Kipling called the

> . . . heathen heart that puts her trust
> In reeking tube and iron shard—

without seeing that as a nation and as individuals we are
terribly tempted to worship the gods of our enemies.

If this were a public meeting and some orator were ex-
horting you with all your might to fight the Nazis, you would
think that patriotic. Well, this is a Christian service, and I
too am pleading that with all our strength we withstand
naziism, but on a level of thought deeper than the clash of
armies, and with a scope that will far outlast the war and de-
termine our children's destiny for years to come. We must not
become what the Nazis are and worship the Nazi gods—the
belief that might makes right, the imperialistic greed that
wants to dominate the world, the ancient heathen tribal deities
of master races and domineering nations. If ever the world
needed faith in the Christian God, one and universal, no re-
specter of persons, before whom all souls are equal, and in
whose sight only justice and goodwill to all can stand, it is
today. If we surrender him to the gods of our enemies, we
shall have lost the war indeed, and then the peace.

When the "Gripsholm" came back on its last trip, a reporter asked one of the missionaries who had been weeks in
a Japanese concentration camp, "What did you think about
while you were imprisoned?" To which he answerd, "I spent
such time as I had to think wondering whether I would be
worthy of freedom when I got it." We need now to think
about that. To conquer the Nazis and then to become Nazis
ourselves—slaves of a state, ridden by passion and prejudice,
the God of Christ displaced by tribal deities—that would be
defeat indeed. Why seek we after the gods of the people, who
have not delivered their own people out of our hands?

Why Is God Silent While Evil Rages?

NO THOUGHTFUL person can live through an era like this without asking searching questions about God. With no desire and no intention to be atheists, still, questions rise within us and among them inevitably this: Why is God so silent in a world filled with noisy evil? We hear, as though it were a lovely truth, that amid earthquake, wind, and fire ravaging the world, God moves like a still, small voice, but far from being a lovely truth, that is what often troubles us. Why, in a world of turbulent evil, can God the Almighty do no better than be a still, small voice? Why does he not speak up, and make a noise in the interest of righteousness? So Carlyle, earnest believer though he was, exclaimed once, "God sits in heaven and does nothing," and long before Carlyle the writer of the eighty-third Psalm cried,

> O God, keep not thou silence:
> Hold not thy peace, and be not still, O God.
> For, lo, thine enemies make a tumult.

This contrast between the blatant violence of evil and the quietness of those spiritual forces in which goodness dwells is a mystery. In what contrast stand a thunderstorm and a mother's love—the one obtrusive, boisterous, the other inaudible, imperceptible, save as one quietly listens! Why should evil have thus the advantage of noise, and goodness always be a still, small voice?

This question gains added difficulty when, believing that these spiritual forces have behind them the might and majesty of the Eternal, we bring God in. Why should the sovereign God of all this universe be so shy? Long ago, during the Hebrew Exile, when proud Babylon violently ruled the earth, the Great Isaiah cried, "Verily thou art a God that hidest thyself, O God of Israel, the Saviour."

No one can crowd the explanation of an infinite universe into a finite head, and the full answer to this question we have asked has depths no human plummet fathoms, but surely some things can be said about it. This, I ask of you, to start with, that when I use the word "God" you will not have in your imagination some human picture of him, like a king seated on a throne. Let us begin with something more realistic and indubitable than that! In one sense of the word no one doubts the existence of God, not even one who calls himself an atheist. There is, behind and in this universe, creative power. That is fact, not theory. This world and we within it are the consequence of creative power. In what terms we shall think of that creative power, whether in terms material or spiritual, is a further and momentous question, but it is certain that creative power itself is here. From it, all that is came. In it, all that is exists. Without it, nothing is at all. It is the sovereign, basic, original, indubitable fact.

Yet, strangely enough, we have never heard it. It makes no noise. Upon its cosmic loom it weaves millions of solar systems and swings stars and planets in their courses, but as the nineteenth Psalm says,

> There is no speech nor language;
> Their voice is not heard.

Here, surely, is the place for our thought to start. Theists and atheists alike, we all are in the same boat here: We face a universe whose sovereign creative power is silent.

Today consider some facts about this mysteriously quiet power from which all things come, that, so it seems to me, lead us straight to the truth of our Christian faith.

For example, we face at once a stern and ominous fact: This silent power does do something rigorous and austere— it works inevitable retribution upon evil. Like it or not, in this universe there is what the ancient Greeks called Nemesis —the doom that, however long delayed, falls upon arrogance and cruelty and braggart pride. In our days we shall see that Nemesis again, and when Hitler's nazidom breaks down, old texts will come to mind:

> He hath made a pit, and digged it,
> And is fallen into the ditch which he made.

Just as in the physical realm the noiseless force of gravitation brings inevitable consequence on those who disobey its. laws, so the law-abiding nature of the cosmos silently reveals itself in the moral realm. "Whatsoever a man soweth, that shall he also reap"—that is a metaphor of silence. The processes of growth are quiet; no one can hear that harvest of retribution grow, but grow it does. So, while it is true that God is silent, it is not true that he "sits in heaven and does nothing."

These are highly emotional days, and among the emotions that naturally roil our spirits is the rebellious mood, resentment and complaint directed often against the very things that once we trusted most. Is anyone here so placid and saintly, so little stirred by the brutal evils of our time, that he has felt no rebellion against God himself? Is not God sovereign? Why does he not speak up? See the blatant wrongs that curse the earth! So we complain, as Dr. Moffatt translates our text,

> Keep not still, O God,
> speak, stir, O God!
> Here are thy foes in uproar.

Nevertheless, any way we look at it, the determining creative forces in this universe are silent, and one major thing they do is noiselessly to work inevitable retribution. Recall the Bible's dramatic presentation of this truth! The Jewish Exile was at its climax. Babylon ruled the world. Then

Belshazzar, the king, made a great feast to a thousand of his lords, where they drank wine and praised the gods of gold and of silver, of brass, of iron, of wood and of stone, until upon that scene of insolent evil a sudden silence fell. For out of the unseen and the unheard there "came forth the fingers of a man's hand, and wrote over against the candlestick upon the plaster of the wall of the king's palace: . . . MENE, MENE, TEKEL, UPHARSIN"—weighed, weighed in the balances and found wanting. "Then the king's countenance was changed . . . and his thoughts troubled him; and the joints of his loins were loosed, and his knees smote one against another."

As Theodor Mommsen, the historian, wrote: "History has a Nemesis for every sin." God does not sit in heaven and do nothing. We frail human beings are not alone the originators, improvisers, and backers of goodness in this world. There is, as Matthew Arnold said, a "power, not ourselves, which makes for righteousness." Today we deeply need to believe that. Evil towers so high, seems so strong, makes such a tumult, that we could easily despair were not our hope still where the great souls of other days have found it. Long ago a valiant warrior against a tyrant cried, "The stars in their courses fought against Sisera," and on the threshold of our own era a modern echoed him:

> And for the everlasting right
> The silent stars are strong.

Come further, now, and consider that despite our complaints about God's silence, these spiritual forces making no noise reach deeper, take hold harder, and last longer than any others. We human beings are naturally sensitive to noise. Loud things claim our attention. Yet, when we go deeply within ourselves to note what means most to us, how soon we enter a quiet realm where great thoughts walk with still feet, and great loves feel what they cannot say, and great faiths lift their noiseless aspirations! The creative factors in our lives dwell in the realm of silence. It is there that personally we meet the Eternal. In these days, filled with the din of man's brutality, we need to renew our insight into the reality, the creative power, the abiding persistence, the ultimate dominance of these quiet spiritual forces that are God's still, small voice.

Even as cold-blooded history reveals the truth, what is it that lasts? All that made a noise in ancient Greece is gone, but the *Iliad*, the *Odyssey*, the *Dialogues of Plato*, the dream of beauty and the love of truth—these have not gone. All that made a noise in ancient Israel has vanished, even the Temple with not one stone left upon another; but the faiths of the psalmists and the insights of the prophets—they have not vanished. How will the atheist handle this realistic fact, that, not because of anything man alone plans to do or is capable of doing, but because of the nature of things, there is a power here that, dropping out the stentorian, vociferous things that split the eardrums of contemporaries, preserves the quiet, spiritual forces, so that while empires rise and fall, truths that hardly lift their voices go on and on.

> Egypt's might is tumbled down
>   Down a-down the deeps of thought;
> Greece is fallen and Troy town,
> Glorious Rome hath lost her crown,
>   Venice' pride is nought.
>
> But the dreams their children dreamed
>   Fleeting, unsubstantial, vain,
> Shadowy as the shadows seemed,
> Airy nothing, as they deemed,
>   These remain.

Moreover, far from being merely a historic matter, this truth has important applications to our times. We are dreadfully tempted now to trust the noisy, outward, violent forces to achieve our end. Many, for example, discussing a new society of nations, say, This time we will have an international police force and that will keep order and make the thing go. Now, I agree that some form of internationally used force is necessary, but if we trust that to hold a society of nations together, we have lost our game before we start. An expert on police affairs recently said that in the United States with our 135,000,000 citizens we have about 150,000 policemen all told, and that no more than 50,000 of them are on duty at any one time. Is it 50,000 policemen who keep this nation a nation and preserve order among 135,000,000 citizens? Granted, the necessity of police to handle the fringes of criminal disorder, what keeps us together, makes of us a loyal, devoted, and on the whole united nation is not something you can put in uniform and arm with a gun. These coherent forces that make of our communities decent places to live in and of America a cooperative people are spiritual. Quiet as the sun that when it rises makes no noise, but that is still the light of all our seeing and the creator of all that grows strong and beautiful, some spiritual faiths and hopes, loves and loyalties, have shined upon us here to make possible our national family. Do we think an international family is possible without that? Any decent world we ever get must be grounded in, buttressed by, and held together with, intelligent, undiscourageable goodwill.

This is not poetry but political realism. Harold Butler was for years Director of the International Labor Office in Geneva under the League of Nations. Listen, then, as he sums up what he regards as the cause of the League's failure: "More than for any other reason the peace was lost because the policies of nations were empty of charity towards each other." All history is a running commentary on that.

How can the atheist handle this fact that the most powerful, creative, persistent forces in human life are spiritual, and that always when the earthquake, wind and fire have spent their force the still, small voice is there?

Come a step further now and note that God may be silent

[168]

but that he or someone mighty like him does do marvelous things in this world. Alike the ultimate mystery and glory of human life is great personality, and you cannot get that out of noisy things. At the age of forty-three Louis Pasteur was a humiliated wreck. One whole side paralyzed, he looked impotently on while war ravaged France, and his fellow-townsmen taunted him with being a useless mouth eating needed food, so that once, grown man though he was, he came home weeping with the sting of their jibes. Yet now when all that made the big noise is gone, Pasteur towers higher every year. Even on that day when he wept for shame he said to his wife, "I have something to give France that men with swords cannot give." Well, inwardly sustained by the disinterested love of truth, he gave it, and years afterwards, he himself explained his own experience as he understood it: "Christ," he said, "made me what I am." How does an atheist deal with such facts—this indubitable presence of silent spiritual power, transforming, sustaining, illumining, the builder and maker of great souls? Believe me, God does not sit in heaven and do nothing!

Moreover, this is not merely an individual matter. These souls, from Elijah to Pasteur, nourished on the still, small voice, lift the world. Even in the physical cosmos the silent force of gravitation is a deep mystery, but not so deep a mystery as the gravitation by which strong souls lift the world. Long ago on Calvary the violent forces of the age successfully engineered a crucifixion. They finished him off, the Man of Nazareth who troubled them, and Pilate and Caiaphas and all the noisy crowd that had cried "Crucify him" went home content, while there he hung, a man condemned, dying a felon's death. In any world whose creative power is merely materialistic, would not that have been indeed the end, that man extinguished like a blown-out candle, his light forever gone? Instead, Pilate and Caiaphas and the shouting crowds are dead and buried in reproach and shame, and that man they crucified is lifting still, with a silent gravitation that will out-last the noisiest earthquakes that ever shake the world.

To be sure, this does present a problem. The least important and least valuable things are the noisiest and thus the most easily perceived and proved, while the most important and most valuable things are hardest to be absolutely sure about. One cannot doubt a thunderstorm; one cannot doubt a war—see the noise they make! But love and liberty and truth and the profoundest meanings and values of our souls—men can doubt them. One cannot doubt an air raid siren—what a blare it makes! But one can doubt God, for he is a still, small voice. This is a mystery and a problem, but thus to state the problem frankly is in part to solve it. Think of being a man who goes through life believing in only the least important and least valuable things because they are obvious and noisy! Fish, they say, in a quiet lake do not recognize the existence of water because they live and move and have their being in it. Shall we, like them, be so insensitive and not perceive that the silent forces of the Eternal Spirit, whose noiseless presence is the life of all our being, are real?

I do not pretend to understand the full reason why God so hides himself in quietness. Perhaps it is because if he should speak out with all the thundering compulsion of his power, making himself as terribly evident as we sometimes wish he would, we would be utterly overborne, helpless automatons with no freedom to make our doing of his will a voluntary choice. But whatever the reason for his silent method, it does not mean that he is doing nothing. Everything in this universe that does most is silent.

> What tho', in solemn silence, all
> Move round the dark terrestrial ball?
> What tho' no real voice nor sound
> Amidst their radiant orbs be found?
> In reason's ear they all rejoice,
> And utter forth a glorious voice,

> Forever singing as they shine,
> "The hand that made us is divine."

As for the personal conclusion of the matter, that surely is evident. In days like these we need the inward reinforcement of spiritual power, and nothing noisy can supply it. There are families here whose anxious thoughts follow their deepest loves to the ends of the earth today. There are homes here where already the War Department's fateful announcement has arrived with news more difficult to meet than any that they ever faced before. And all of us, tossed by the turbulence and wearied with the din of this violent time, need to have our souls restored. But thundering airplanes and falling bombs do not restore the soul, no, nor clanging subways, shouting crowds, and all the blaring noises of our busy days. As God lives his deepest life in silence, so do we. It is when our quiet responds to his quiet that we find him. Only when he leads us in green pastures and beside still waters can he restore our souls.

And when from that silent place one who knows its secret goes out again to face the world, not all its din can overawe his spirit. The destiny of creation is in the hand of forces that make no noise. So, from the complaint of one psalmist we turn to the insight of another who heard the Eternal say, "Be still, and know that I am God."

No Dry-as-Dust Religion Will Do Now

NO MERELY formal, routine religion can help a man much in these days. Many of us must acknowledge, however, that our own personal experience of Christianity has often been conventional—inherited beliefs passively accepted, or opinions into which superficially we have argued ourselves, or observances of worship on which we were brought up. Much so-called Christianity is thus secondhand and dry as dust.

Over against such formalism we set today the experience of the blind man whom Jesus healed and who in the face of attack and denial stood up for something he felt sure about: "One thing I know, that, whereas I was blind, now I see." That is the genuine article in spiritual experience—a man seeing something so clearly that nothing can make him deny it.

No one need be troubled by the miracle involved in this narrative if he does not wish to be. The writer of the Fourth Gospel was primarily a preacher, presenting Jesus as vividly as he knew how as the life-giver—that is what the story of the raising of Lazarus is all about; and as the light-bringer—that is what the healing of this blind man is about. It is the spiritual meaning, reproducible in us, that John is mainly driving at, as in this parable-story he portrays a man born blind who at last can see, and who at that point stands his ground against all comers; when even the religious leaders of his people argue with him, cajole him, threaten him, he digs his heels in and will not budge. Jesus, he says, may be this or that, and your opinions may be thus or so, but one thing I personally know: "Whereas I was blind, now I see." That, says the Fourth Gospel, is a bona fide spiritual experience.

Thus to pass from blindness to sight is a true and vivid

way of picturing radical personal transformation. Once on an autumn day when the Swiss forests were glorious with lavish intermarriages of color I stood on an Alpine height with one of the grandest views on earth outspread before me, when two women came toiling up, stared listlessly around, and said, "We heard that there is a view up here. Where is it?" So, at secondhand they were thinking of something Baedeker had starred—conventional believers in what someone else had reported he had seen. But what if their eyes could have been opened? So,

> Earth's crammed with heaven,
> And every common bush afire with God:
> But only he who sees, takes off his shoes.

Throughout the New Testament the Christian faith is thus presented in terms of vision. We Christians are sometimes accused of blind faith, and much in the church's history justifies the charge, but blind faith is a travesty on what the New Testament celebrates. From Jesus saying, "Blessed are the pure in heart: for they shall see God," to Paul rejoicing because the eyes of our hearts can be enlightened, the New Testament is a running commentary on this story in John's Gospel, its great souls standing their ground against the pagan degradation of their times with the conviction of those who have seen something so clearly that they cannot deny it.

Consider, to start with, that the lack of this quality in our experience springs in part from our capacity theoretically to believe so many things that we do not really see. We believe in many Christian opinions; we inherited them; they are starred in the Baedeker of our Western tradition; but what we really see in life is something else altogether. We are often like the cat in the Mother Goose rhyme who went up to London to see the queen:

> Pussy-cat, pussy-cat, what did you there?
> I frightened a little mouse under the chair.

[173]

That is exactly what a cat would do in the presence of the queen—see a mouse; and what either cat or man thus vividly sees in life is far more influential than anything theoretically believed.

The common saying runs that seeing is believing. To be sure it is, but the reverse is not true. Believing is not necessarily seeing. Some of us for years believed that the Yosemite Valley was beautiful, and then one day we saw. Some of us long believed that true love might be what Mrs. Browning in her sonnets sang concerning it, and then one day we saw. Some of us believed for years that there must be solid experience behind the psalmist's words,

Though I walk through the valley of the shadow of death,
I will fear no evil; for thou art with me,

and then one day we saw. Believing is not necessarily seeing. Believing may be a conventional substitute for seeing, a mere acceptance of what someone else reports that he has seen.

We Christians say that we believe in Jesus Christ. How little that may matter to personal character and social conduct the sad story of Christendom makes plain. Doubtless we do believe in Jesus Christ. Why should we not? So men who themselves never have a gleam of scientific insight can believe that Thomas Edison was a great scientist. So folk who themselves get nothing from music can believe that Toscanini is a great musician. How superficial belief can be! But one thing would not be superficial. To see life as Jesus saw it, perceive in it what he beheld there, look at people, and money, and friendship, and trouble, and death as he looked at them—that would not be superficial. That would start going again an old way of confessing faith which once was the life of the gospel, but too seldom is heard in our modern churches: "One thing I know, that, whereas I was blind, now I see."

Consider further that this gift of vision was the aim of

Jesus' ministry. Zacchæus the tax-gatherer, the woman of Samaria, Mary Magdalene, and all the rest, had seen life one way before they met Jesus, but afterwards they could never see it so again. Thus William Dean Howells ran upon Tolstoy and wrote to a friend: "I can never again see life in the way I saw it before I knew him."

We must have known some such experience—looking at life one way today, and then, suddenly it may be, meeting somebody who opens our eyes, changes our point of view, clarifies our vision so that we never again see things as we saw them before. That was Jesus' effect on the first disciples. He opened their eyes to a new way of looking at life.

In this regard Jesus was an artist, for this is what an artist does. He does not argue; he piles up no accumulating mass of evidence to the smashing climax of a Q.E.D. which will compel consent. An artist's method is different. He paints a picture, and says, See! He writes a poem, and says, See!

So Jesus seldom, if ever, argued. One of the astonishing things about his ministry is that though his life has been immeasurably influential upon the thinking of mankind, from one end of the Gospels to the other you will hardly find an argument upon his lips. He told the story of the Prodigal coming back from a Far Country and of the difference in attitude between the father and the churlish elder brother, and he said, Do you see? He told a story of five wise maidens who went to a wedding feast while there still was time, and of five foolish ones who procrastinated until they discovered that there is such a thing as being too late, and he said, Do you see? In a single sentence he summed up a wide area of man's experience, saying, "A man's life consisteth not in the abundance of the things which he possesseth," and he said, Do you not see? He told the story of a Good Samaritan who helped a stranger in his need, and he asked, Can you not see?

If he had only argued with us we could have answered him. We have wits for arguing; we know the tricks of the debater.

We could have replied to him, argument for argument. But what shall we do with one who tells stories, paints pictures, uses metaphors, sums up age-long experience in flashing sentences, with that unescapable refrain, Do you see?—when at our best we do see, know that he is right, know that we ought to look at life as he looked at it, and that all talk about merely believing in him is nothing if we do not share his seeing.

If someone is tempted to say, Yes, Jesus was artistic but not scientific, I answer, To be sure Jesus was not scientific, not because he was unscientific but because he was something else altogether—an artist. Note, however, that the climax of all science, too, is seeing. The hour when Galileo with the eye of his mind saw the planets moving about the sun, the hour when Newton with the eye of his imagination saw apple and star under one law—such supreme turning points in science's history too are hours of insight and vision, and there and everywhere the future of mankind depends upon people who can say, "Whereas I was blind, now I see."

How real an experience that is, and what solid substance it puts into Christianity if that is what it means! Listen to this from a character in a popular play: "What can I say?" she ejaculates. "I've said it all. Nothing matters but happiness. Get your share. Life's a racket; loyalty's a joke. We've debunked everything but lust." That does not sound like a creed, but it is, for a creed is nothing if it is not a way of seeing life.

Turn from that to Jesus, and how profound the difference! He looked on people, and behind the leprosy of the leper, the sin of the sinner, the poverty of the poor, he turned on every personality he met his creatively seeing eyes. He looked on friendship, so easily taking the tarnish of a selfish world, and what he saw we never can forget: "Greater love hath no man than this, that a man lay down his life for his friends." He looked on money, which readily becomes a god for the sake of whom men sell their souls, and what he saw haunts us yet in all our nobler hours: "What shall it profit a man, if he shall gain the whole world, and lose his own soul?" He looked on the sins that men make game of, excuse themselves for with glib and easy phrases, upon the lusts that always involve another person, the selfishness that always hurts another person, the infidelity that always betrays another person, and what he saw stripped from sin all drapery and left the naked fact that sin is conduct that makes it hard for other persons to live well. He looked on death and said, "Be not afraid of them that kill the body, and after that have no more that they can do." And he looked on beauty, too, on Galilean flowers, and little children, and fathers who forgave their sons, and in all life's goodness he saw the revelation of Eternal God at the heart of things. That is bona fide, genuine Christianity— nothing formal and dry-as-dust about it, but seeing life as Jesus saw it.

With this in mind let us come to our own selves in these troublous days and emphasize the fact that no other kind of religion except this can meet our present need. So large a company could not be gathered without some here being tempted, as many in our day are tempted, to give up religion and get on without it. Granted, that we can get on without some kinds of religion. In a generation so momentous, why one should waste time on the credulities and sectarianisms that commonly pass for religion, I cannot comprehend. Lloyd George was one day driving through North Wales with a friend and the talk turned to denominational differences. "The church I belong to," said Lloyd George, "is torn with a fierce dispute. One section says that baptism is *in* the name of the Father, and the other that it is *into* the name of the Father. I belong to one of these parties. I feel most strongly about it. I would die for it in fact—but I forget which it is!" I should say so! When, however, one is finished with all that, clean done and impatiently through with the trivialities and obscurantisms of conventional faith, one still faces the fact that nothing makes more difference than the way one sees life. To see life as Nietzsche saw it and as Hitler sees it, or to see life as Christ sees it—what a difference! No one in his senses can say that that does not matter.

War does strange things to religion. It makes some people fundamentalists. Fundamentalism always has a revival in wartime, and for an obvious reason. When everything is shaken, chaotic, and insecure, the psychological effect on some is to make them turn back to old ideas that seem familiar and stable, and so in wartime the fundamentalists revive, vehemently insisting on ancient dogmas long overpassed by modern knowledge, seeking security there where no real security is. Others are driven by war to a superstitious faith, a religion of magic that in a desperate predicament reaches wildly out for almost any kind of superhuman help. As the chaplains say, one reason why there is no atheism in the fox-holes is that in the fox-holes the situation is so terrific that one desperately grasps at any reassurance one can find. As for the civilian population, emergency religion thrives; folk turn even to the churches, seeking it, as when a man adrift at sea lays hold on any piece of floating wreckage he can get his hand on. Such crisis-religion is easily understood, but it does not go deep. So on the walls of a certain physician's office hangs this quatrain:

> God and the doctor, all men adore
> When sickness comes, but not before;
> When health returns, alike requited,
> God is forgotten and the doctor slighted!

Today we are pleading for something more intelligent than fundamentalism and more profound and real than emergency religion. An era like this ought to open our eyes until we see things we never saw before. Sometime since, the Archbishop of Canterbury, addressing the students of Oxford University, said: "The world, as we live in it, is like a shop window in which some mischievous person has got in overnight and shifted all the price labels round, so that the cheap things have the high-price labels on them and the really precious things are priced low." Then he added, "We let ourselves be taken in." So! We let ourselves be taken in! We see the precious as cheap, and the cheap as precious. What if out of this wartime experience we could come with our eyes opened, henceforth like that blind man to speak with personal conviction about some great and central matters on which man's destiny depends: "One thing I know, that, whereas I was blind, now I see."

Permit me a moment of autobiography, for this kind of experience saved my own Christian faith and led me into the ministry. In my youth the time came when the formal creeds to me were dust and ashes. I did not believe them. How could I go into the ministry so? Yet, in the Christian gospel I did see something—only a little, to be sure, but at least that much I personally saw—and now with gratitude I look back on the day when I made the greatest venture of my life: I can preach what I see—that was the way I had to start. God helping me, I said, I will never preach what I do not see, but what I see I can say. It seemed so little to go on at first, because I saw so little, yet now an older man I am glad that I humbly joined the great tradition of this blind man, his eyes just opening, much dark to him, much unsure, saying simply, One thing I know, one thing at least, once blind, I see!

Surely I am speaking to someone's personal condition here. You, too, are troubled because in this mysterious world so much is dark to you. Sometimes when you hear great faiths announced, great hymns sung, great Scriptures read, you say, I cannot believe that. My friend, on that account do not, I beg of you, shut yourself out of the Christian heritage. Some of the most moving faith in history has been like the faith of this blind man—humble, simple, nothing stereotyped or conventional about it, restricted in scope, not claiming to know everything, but what there was of it bona fide and vital: One thing I know, one thing, once blind, I see. Did not Jesus mean this when he said that if a man have faith as a grain of mustard seed—little indeed, but alive, vital, real—he may yet move mountains? Start where you are, my friend, with what you do see; be true to that, and so go on to see more as this blind man did, to whom Jesus in the end said: "Dost thou believe on the Son of God? He answered and said, And who is he, Lord, that I may believe on him? Jesus said unto him, Thou hast both seen him, and he it is that speaketh with thee. And he said, Lord, I believe. And he worshipped him."

Today we face not only military but spiritual enemies, who do more than theoretically believe something. They see life in terms that mean its enslavement and its moral ruin, and they can be met only by a truer way of seeing life. Listen to another story from the Gospels. Jesus answered Bartimæus and said: "What wilt thou that I should do unto thee? And the blind man said unto him, Rabboni, that I may receive my sight."

Keeping Faith in Persuasion in a World of Coercion

JOHN'S Gospel in its twelfth chapter reports that Jesus said about his crucifixion, "I, if I be lifted up from the earth, will draw all men unto me." The Master, that is, trusted his cause to the power of persuasion. He lacked both the desire and the opportunity to compel anyone. Whatever consequence was to come from his ministry could come only from the appeal of his life and love and sacrifice, drawing to himself men's voluntary allegiance. The amazing thing is that he trusted in that.

A contrast of immense import confronts us at Calvary—on the one side the Roman Empire, one of the mightiest concentrations of compulsive power in history, and on the other, Jesus, saying, Lift me up, even though it be upon a cross; make visible this quality of life and love and sacrifice, and in the long run man's heart will be won by it, will respond to it, and I will draw all men unto me. How could he so trust the power of voluntary persuasion against the vast might of an empire's coercion?

Theoretically we know that this is the essence of the Christian gospel—Christ lifted up in the faith that deep in man are capacities to see his glory, respond to his quality, be moved by his self-sacrifice, until mankind is won in voluntary allegiance to his discipleship. But today prodigious facts seem to make nonsense of all that, in a world trusting above all else in coercive violence. Who is not tempted at times to cry, Ah, Christ, two thousand years ago you were lifted up, but mankind has proved more obdurate than you supposed—humanity has not responded in gratitude and devotion to your appeal! Did not you yourself speak of casting pearls before swine? So it has turned out, your hopes vain that there is in man

[181]

at large willingness to answer your love with responsive love and your sacrifice with grateful self-surrender. Mankind is a tougher proposition than such idealistic faith supposes, and now not persuasion but coercion rules the world!

Were this a sociological classroom we would discuss the relative place of these two major forces, persuasion and coercion, in any society, and we would say of course that both are necessary. No ordered society can exist without coercion. In both Jeremiah and the Psalms is a sobering figure of speech: "Adders, . . . which will not be charmed." As the psalmist puts it:

> Their venom [is] like a viper's;
>   they are deaf as any cobra,
> that will not listen to the charmer's voice,
>   to the most cunning spell.

Even the ancient snake charmer with his strange power over serpents found some serpents obdurate to his persuasion. In every society there are such. Visit some courtroom where little children and the fathers who have beaten them are brought in. If anyone can love and forgive beyond limit, it is a little child, and these children have so forgiven and so loved again the brutal men whose rage has been vented on their defenseless bodies; yet, hardened against this most persuasive appeal that can play upon the human heart, these men have gone on beating the scarred bodies of their own children. There are "adders, . . . which will not be charmed," and so of course coercion must step in. As far ahead as we can see, in all societies, national and international, coercion will be needed.

Today everyone is emphasizing that. Our ears are filled with the din of its reiteration, and the earth shakes with the impact of its practice. Our inner personal difficulty lies not in seeing the necessity of coercion but in maintaining in a violent era, when coercion has gone mad, our faith in persuasion, too. Our problem is to remain Christian through all this exaltation of force, not losing sight of that realm of truth in which the Master trusted. And if someone protests, But you just have said that this trust of his has failed, I reply, The Roman Empire that Jesus faced was a concentration of coercive might unsurpassed in history, and it fell long ago; but he is here, and when all the empires now locked in violent struggle have fallen too, he will be here still, persuasively drawing men to himself. What if in the long run persuasion is mightier and more enduring than coercion?

To start with, it certainly is true that whatever is finest in our own characters came by that method. Our real goodness was not flogged into us but was drawn out in us by the appeal of something lovely and right to which we responded. Our fathers and mothers used coercion so slightly that we have now forgotten it, but that other power they wielded we have not forgotten—the day by day appeal of life and love, of character and sacrifice that, falling on us like the sunshine, called out our best. Remember our first meeting with great music when something within us responded, saying, That belongs to me and I to it; or our reading of some great book to which our minds and emotions answered; or our hero-worship of some character of whom we felt, I had rather be like that than anything else in the world; and from those early days till now, not by compulsion but by persuasion our best has come. We cannot make living things grow with a sledge hammer no matter how hard we pound.

Moreover, this truth about our personal lives has far-reaching social consequence. Today our attention is centered on embattled nations and our hearts are shaken by a world at war, until coercion seems everything. But when these imperial defeats and triumphs have become historic, and new world setups have altered beyond our recognition the boundaries of nations, three social institutions will still be here, man's hope of all the character the world can count upon—homes, schools, and churches—and these three are institutions not of coercion

[183]

but of persuasion. A good home or school uses a minimum of compulsion and a maximum of persuasion, and a church has no compulsion at all at its disposal, only persuasion to rely upon. Yet, age after age, while empires rise and fall, these three go on—homes, schools, churches—the major builders of man's goodness. What if the Master's insight was profounder far than the disciples of coercion understand?

All the progress mankind has ever made has sprung from the victories of persuasion over coercion. Not only in good homes, good schools, good churches, but in democracy against tyranny, in free research against the shackling of men's minds, in ethical liberty against compulsive codes, in civilized society where violence has given way to law—always, progress means that coercion has been pushed back, and persuasion has won a wider field. And wherever that happens, it means too that there must be more and more individual men and women who do not need to be compelled, whose goodness is voluntary, who are right from within because they have seen something everlastingly worth while lifted up, and have responded to it.

Granted, the adders that cannot be charmed, on whom coercion must be used. Granted, that Tennyson was much too optimistic when he wrote,

> We needs must love the highest when we see it,
> Not Lancelot, nor another.

Alas, we can refuse to "love the highest when we see it"! But it is still true that the kind of character that can move this world one inch forward comes only, as Jesus said, in men and women voluntarily persuaded by, and inwardly drawn to, something high and lifted up.

Come further now and see that this insight of Jesus applies in a realm where least of all today we are inclined to believe it; we never really conquer anyone until we conquer him by persuasion.

For society's protection we lock up one of these human

adders that cannot be charmed, and there in the penitentiary he sits, embittered, rebellious, angry, cursing God and man. We were right to lock him up, but obviously he has not been conquered. If, however, in the hands of some wise penologist, a persuasive, understanding goodwill can be so brought to bear on him that he inwardly surrenders to a way of living that makes him not an adder but a man, then society has really conquered him. In the slums of London General Booth of the Salvation Army dealt with a hardened character who believed in neither God nor goodness and who after endless run-ins with the police was still an obdurate and sullen soul. But one day after months of patient dealing, General Booth saw that man's citadel surrender, so that he was really conquered. "Love and kindness," he said as he broke down before the General's goodwill, "Love and kindness! Then there really is a God!"

This truth we are driving at we know well when we apply it to ourselves. What does it take to conquer us? Let any man or nation try it by coercion and he will see how still unconquered our souls will be. Deprived of outward liberty, crushed by military power, we might be, but our inner citadels would be uncaptured and our rebellious souls unconquered still. Think of the millions in Europe today outwardly defeated but inwardly unsubdued, and consider this mystery, that not all the coercion in the world can really conquer a strong soul. It takes something mightier than coercion to do that; it takes persuasion. For there are times when our inner citadels throw wide their doors to let a conqueror in. We surrender—and it is our glory—to something or someone we are persuaded we rightfully belong to, and we make a festival of our capitulation.

> Lift up your heads, O ye gates;
> And be ye lifted up, ye everlasting doors:
> And the King of glory will come in.

That alone is the real conquest of a soul, and no compulsion ever does it.

What is true of souls is true of nations, and in this violent era we need to grasp that fact. All the world is set on conquest, and we deeply need to see what conquering means. To defeat a nation with our armies and leave it crushed, rebellious, resentful, angry, is not to conquer it. It will not stay defeated so. We ourselves would not so stay defeated. Real conquering is ultimately a spiritual matter, the inner conquest of a nation by the persuasive forces of justice, fair play, goodwill, until the nation's soul voluntarily surrenders to a world policy that is good for all. Here lies the ultimate futility of war, that when its devastating violence has run its course, the major problems it started out to solve are still unsolved, because no violence can solve them. So Abraham Lincoln said: "Suppose you go to war, you cannot fight always; and when, after much loss on both sides, and no gain on either, you cease fighting, the identical old questions as to terms of intercourse are again upon you." Like it or not, to every powerful nation in the world Mrs. Browning's words have today become practical politics:

> Why, conquering
> May prove as lordly and complete a thing
> In lifting upward as in crushing low.

We are not talking now about appeasement. Appeasement is an absurd policy—throwing a bone to a dog in the hope that if the dog gets that bone he will not want another. Appeasement can be selfish in motive, and it is futile in outcome. Rather we are thinking about the kind of conquering that lasts, and whether it be ourselves or Germany, Japan or Russia, no nation is ever really conquered until it is spiritually won.

Our President's reiterated plea that we must win not only the war but the peace involves this. Armies and navies can win the war, but they cannot win the peace, and as one sees the pick of our youth torn from their vocational ambitions and their domestic hopes and plunged into this holocaust, who does not feel that not to win the peace would be the most awful betrayal that any generation could perpetrate upon its youth?

> The many men, so beautiful!
> And they all dead did lie:
> And a thousand thousand slimy things
> Lived on; and so did I.

We saw that happen after the last war; we do not want to see it again. The winning of the peace, however, involves the triumph of persuasive forces. It means at the first chance feeding the hungry, rehabilitating the devastated countries, opening economic doors of hope to stricken people, through organized goodwill trying to undo the appalling evils of military conquest by another kind of conquest altogether: winning enemies to be friends, turning wartime belligerents into peacetime co-operators. And at the earliest possible moment—the sooner the better—it means too an honest plan of world organization whose justice and fair play will make surrender to it an honorable act for any nation. If we are going to win the peace, we must count upon the persuasive forces.

One of the marvels of Abraham Lincoln's career was the way, amid the cruel necessities of war, he kept this kind of insight clear. At the height of the Civil War, when feeling was bitterest, he dropped one day at a White House reception a hopeful remark about the South, and an elderly woman flared up at him, wanting to know how he could speak kindly of his enemies when he should wish above all else to destroy them. And the record runs that Lincoln answered, "What, madam? do I not destroy them when I make them my friends?" Granted, the stern necessities of immediate action that confront us, that outlook of Lincoln is the long view. No mere crushing of a nation, however much its leadership needs to be crushed, constructively solves the main, long-range problem. Only the final saving of the nations, the ultimate transformation of them from enmity to friendship, the incorporation of them, at last, in the human family—only that is intelligent and creative realism.

This whole range of truth, applicable alike to our private and public life, applies with urgent criticalness to our churches in wartime. Whatever other function the church of Christ may have, this is central and mandatory—to keep faith in persuasion in a world of coercion. The church, too, in days of political power, has tried its hand at coercive violence, endeavoring to make men Christian by force, but the memory of such persecuting zeal is now infamous—the crusades no longer holy and where Calvin burned Servetus at the stake an expiatory monument erected by Calvinists. Today, however, the church is tempted to an appalling substitute for its old violence—not, indeed, waging war itself but blessing it, giving war its sanction and backing, and even giving it the Lord's sanction and backing, too. So, deserting its God-given function, the church forgets to be the church, and instead of presenting to the world an international, interracial fellowship relying on the power of persuasion, it is tempted to let the various nations take possession of it, dictate its message, make of it a sponsor of war's brutality until its voice is indistinguishable from all the other voices that cry up the war.

To be sure, it is tragically difficult for individuals and churches to be Christian in wartime. War presents to the Christian conscience an intolerable dilemma, and no matter what attitude one takes—pacifist or non-pacifist—one faces the inner agony of self-contradiction. To be sure the churches cannot separate themselves from their people and their nation; despite themselves they are in the war; they must follow their sons and daughters into all the hells that war produces; and in a world where the Christian method of persuasion is understood, believed in, and responded to by so few, it is insane to expect the policies of nations at this present time to be controlled by it. Still, as of old and for how long time ahead only heaven knows, Pascal's words describe the situation: "Because men do not fortify justice, they justify force." All this is true—so true that Christians who still maintain their faith in the power of persuasion as the ultimate hope of the world may expect the jibes of the contemptuous even among their own brethren. They are sure to be caricatured as "the lads who think that if they smile long enough they will get an answering smile back again." Well, when Jesus set his straight course, trusting in the persuasiveness of spiritual forces, he expected few smiles back again; he expected what he got, the cross; but it has turned out to be the strongest lifting power in history.

Difficult it is for individuals and churches to be Christian in wartime, but this does not dispense the church from its obligation to its special function. Even our persecuting forefathers saw *that*, and when they burned a heretic they turned the ungodly task over to "the secular arm" of the state. That legalistic trick deceives no one now and lifts no shame from the churchmen who used it; nor will it relieve us of any burden of responsibility, if, blessing war, becoming part and parcel of it, our voices indistinguishable from others in its support, we turn over to "the secular arm" the task that we are sanctioning.

Even amid the passions of war, with all the realistic facts that make personal neutrality impossible and constrain us, now that war is here, emphatically to desire victory for one side rather than the other, let the Christian church still be the Christian church and not something else! Once more preachers are tempted to present arms in honor of war. Listen, however, to an American reporter in Burma:

The human wreckage from last night's terrible action has come in and is still coming in and the place is a shambles of

screaming and groaning men, of stumps of limbs and buckets
of flesh, of horrible things with half-faces and half-bodies, of
things that you feel it is a pity to keep alive, of men dying
on the four constantly filled operating tables, of things under
sheets that you would not dare lift up for fear of going mad,
of wounded lying half-covered in pools of muddy rain water
because there is no place to put them and no time to make any
place, and through it all the doctors and nurses moving and
working as though in a daze, as though in a horrible trance,
until you walk away from it sick at your stomach and wishing
to God you had never gone near it.

That is war. As for war's wider aspects we need new metaphors and similes. We still use ancient figures of speech with
no relevance to modern facts. We say we "draw the sword,"
but when we moderns go to war we do not draw the sword.
We start a forest fire that stops at nothing, spares nobody,
destroys everything.

Over against all this stands the essential message and
method of the Christian gospel—Christ, lifted up and drawing men to him. If a man thinks it mad to trust the power of
such persuasion as our ultimate hope, let him say so! But let
him recognize that in saying so he denies the Christian gospel
at its very heart!

The deepest difference separating churchmen today is not
doctrinaire pacifism versus doctrinaire non-pacifism, but the
contrast between those who, war or no war, are trying to
keep the church true to its essential message and its special
function, and those who are surrendering the church's distinctive gospel to the passions of the time. Not less but more
because violent coercion is now predominant, the church's
long-range, abiding message needs to be maintained. If we do
not maintain it, who will? In the end, when violence has spent
its force and left immeasurable chaos in its wake, the world
will come back to that message and method again for anything
creative it wants done. After this war, as after any other, the
world will say once more what Miss Dorothy Thompson—

who is certainly no pacifist—said after the last war: "War has become a greater menace than any enemy can possibly be, and the first call upon our patriotism is to defend ourselves against war itself. . . . If I had children I would tell them just one thing about the last war, and I would tell it to them over and over again: *No nation won it. Every one lost it. And from now on all great wars will always be lost by all the combatants."*

So, in the end, we return to the place we started from—the cross. Men have built complicated theologies about it, and then have waged endless controversies concerning their credibility. It is not the theology of the cross, however, that puts on our faith the heavy strain, but the cross as a way of life, trusting in the power of persuasion though the Roman Empire confront our non-violence with its towering force. Here lies the test of the church's loyalty to the cross, that even in a warring generation it still is sure that the persuasiveness of a divine life, lived sacrificially for men, reaches deeper, takes hold harder, and lasts longer, than all the coercion the world can mass against it.

When Life Reaches Its Depths

THESE are days when our lives do go down into the depths. To be sure, life happily has not only depths but shallows, not only profundities but gaieties. We could not endure life without that. Our thought this morning concerns our more serious moods, but this other side of our nature is important, too—the superficial, if you will, the light-hearted, cheerful and merry.

Obviously this side of our nature finds response from the world without. The gay asks for gaiety and it is answered; the merry mood asks for trivialities and they are there; the shallows call to the shallows and there is response. But surely that alone does not exhaust the meaning of anybody's life. Sometimes life does run out into its depths, and then, when the deep in us calls for something deep to answer it, we face one of life's great hours.

That very phrase comes from the forty-second Psalm. The psalmist's experience had run out into the depths in trouble, and, remembering the thundering cataracts that pour down in springtime from the melting snows of Mount Hermon, and roar, and echo, and answer one another in the gorges beneath, he used that similitude to describe his experiences. "Deep," he said, "calleth unto deep at the noise of thy waterfalls." Every serious life has that experience, where the profundities within ask for an answering profundity. No longer do the shallows suffice. Life within faces some profound abyss of experience, and the deep asks for an answering deep. So when deep calls unto deep and the deep replies, we face the essential experience of religion.

This explains the deathless hold that religious faith has upon the human spirit. Irreligion reduces the world to a fortuitous, self-arrangement of physical elements, and thereby empties the world of the meaning that religious faith finds in God. There is no God, says irreligion, no Divine purpose in life, no goodness beyond our human goodness, no high source for our existence, and no destiny at last except a universal ash heap. Nevertheless, while irreligion thus takes all depth of meaning out of the universe, it leaves man still with the deep in him—depths of trouble, of love, of moral need, of ethical devotion, of spiritual insight—the same old profound experiences that man's nature has known throughout its history. But in irreligion when these deeps within call for a responsive depth, only the shallows are there to answer.

This is the ultimate tragedy of irreligion. I am not saying that all irreligious people must be unhappy. There is much in the world that responds to much that is in them. Their gay moods can be answered by gaieties, their esthetic moods by beauties, their truth-loving moods by science, their affectionate moods by human love—there is much in the world, religion or no religion, to make it interesting and valuable. Yet, when all this is granted, for the thoroughgoing irreligionist a tragedy lies in wait. Some day his life will go out into the depths—profound trouble, profound love, profound moral need, profound ethical devotion, profound spiritual insight—and then the deep will call out for a depth at the heart of life to answer it. And what if there is no deep there!

If this is true in ordinary times, how much more true it is in this, one of the most serious days in man's history! To see how true it is, and how indispensable a matter Christian faith is standing for, consider those hours when life does move out into its depths. For example, in trouble. A man, let us say, has had a smooth and easy life where tragedy has been like a rumor from a far country, but one day a knock comes on his door and tragedy steps in. That experience always adds a new dimension to life, and it is the dimension of depth. "Deep trouble," we say, not broad, long, high—those adjectives would not apply—but "deep trouble." When the psalmist says, "Out of the depths have I cried unto thee, O Lord," we know what he means. He is in trouble. We all enjoy comedy. It is a benediction in a weary hour. The shallow calls to the shallow, and we delight in it. But everyone knows that a tragedy like *Hamlet* goes deeper than comedy.

Each of us has a date with this experience, and when it arrives the psalmist's words come true: "Deep calleth unto deep." For when tragedy faces life one does cry out for something deep to answer it—a faith profound enough to give trouble meaning, and strong enough to sustain one in its endurance. When death takes those we love, when children slip through our arms, when war breaks and catastrophe crashes down and life tumbles in, or when one writes in one's diary what Katherine Mansfield, a brilliant young English author, stricken with tuberculosis, wrote, "There is no limit to human suffering. When one thinks: 'Now I have touched the bottom of the sea—now I can go no deeper,' one goes deeper," then out of the depths the soul cries for answering depths. In such an hour how shallow irreligion is!

One of our contemporary irreligionists says that man has "no reason to suppose that his own life has any more meaning than the life of the humblest insect that crawls from one annihilation to another." So, out of the depths I cry and only the shallows answer—no meaning in life, life coming from nowhere, going nowhither, signifying nothing! As one of our modern poets puts it,

> If after all that we have lived and thought,
> All comes to Nought—
> If there be nothing after Now,
> And we be nothing anyhow,
> And we know that—why live?

In Christian faith, however, the deep in us is not thus answered by the shallows. For when our profundities call out for an answering profundity, Christian faith says, God is there; his eternal purpose comprehends all life; this world is a place for the growing of souls, and in that process adversity is as indispensable as joy; all supreme spirits have come up out of great tribulation; there is power available to enable one to win that victory. So, deep calleth unto deep!

Carry our thought further now and see that in another area life runs out into its depths—not only in trouble but in love. How naturally we say, He is deeply in love! Wherever love is strong and beautiful life reaches its depths. Anyone, for example, who has had a great mother has had one of the unfathomable experiences. Strange how powerfully it keeps its hold long after the mother herself has passed into the invisible! Strange how a man fights his battles out and wins such victories as he is able, and grows old, older far than his mother was when she died, but still feels that to her he owes the major part of everything that he has done. Others might fail him, but she never; others might doubt his possibilities, but she rose on them like the sun and fell on them like the rain, in her encouragement.

Say our worst about human nature, there is in it this depth, the love of fathers and mothers, the love of true friends, the love of true marriage, causing Robert Browning to say to his wife,

> Oh I must feel your brain prompt mine,
>   Your heart anticipate my heart,
> You must be just before, in fine,
>   See and make me see, for your part,
> New depths of the divine!

Say our worst about us humans, we do, like Christ himself, having loved his own, love them unto the end. There is this depth in man!

Now, over against this deep of true love put a summary statement of irreligion by one of its brilliant contemporary devotees: "Living," he says, "is merely a physiological process with only a physiological meaning." How can one believe that? Then the deep of love in man is solitary—nothing at the heart of reality to answer it; it came from nowhere and is going nowhither; it is an accident; when it cries out for the deep there is no deep to respond. That is the tragedy of irreligion.

Indeed, irreligion cannot permanently stand this bafflement, that the profundity in man should be unanswered by a profundity beyond, and so irreligion is irresistibly tempted to depreciate, defame, and at last deny, the profundities in man. If you doubt it, read our irreligious literature, our pagan novelists and essayists. So Professor Edman of Columbia University sums it up: "Love," he says, in much of our current, cynical literature, is represented as "simply lust on parade," and friendship as only "the desire for attention or for praise." Thus the deeps in man are smeared. Love is reduced to sublimated lust; motherhood is reduced to an accidental, biological phenomenon; friendship is reduced to camouflaged homosexuality; and life itself is reduced to merely a physiological process with only a physiological meaning. I am not saying, of course, that every irreligionist explicitly does that, but I am saying that our modern world is shot through and through with a gross, debasing paganism that springs from, and is supported by, such irreligion.

Christian faith does fight an indispensable battle for man's depths. For Christian faith says, Love is real, the divinest reality in the universe; "God is love," "Now abideth faith, hope, love, . . . and the greatest of these is love." That, I am sure, is the only philosophy that can ultimately sustain man's greatness. Alas for souls in whom this deep goes unanswered by any corresponding deep, until at the last they are tempted even to deny the deep within themselves!

Carry our thought further now by noting that life runs out into its depth not simply in trouble and in love but in moral need. Sometime since in a New York hotel a chambermaid one morning found the body of a young man, dead with a bullet hole through his head, and on the dresser his last will and testament lay, written on a sheet of hotel paper: "I leave to society a bad example. I leave to my friends the memory of a misspent life. I leave to my father and mother all the sorrow they can bear in their old age. I leave to my wife a broken heart, and to my children the name of a drunkard and a suicide. I leave to God a lost soul, who has insulted his mercy." That young man had gone into the depths of moral need. Even when it is not so tragic, that experience still is deep. You read detective stories? You are interested in the application of modern science to criminology? It has gotten so now that a man can hardly go into a room without leaving traces of himself. He leaves fingerprints all over. He leaves fibers from his clothes and hairs from his head. Always where he goes he leaves something of himself behind. Man discovers that he does that morally. He leaves his moral fingerprints on everything he touches. He cannot go into a room without leaving his traces. And in hours of penitence he understands what the converted sinner in Masefield's poem meant when he said, "The harm I done by being me."

In such hours of penitence and moral need how utterly shallow irreligion is! Says one of our contemporary irreligionists, "We don't matter. Man matters only to himself. He is fighting a lone fight against a vast indifference." Picture a man in real moral need, the deep crying out for the deep, and nothing there to answer him except a vast indifference! Christian faith is fighting a battle for man's profound experiences, and to anyone here today in moral need it offers no vast indifference as an answer, but forgiveness, a second chance, the possibility of a fresh beginning, reinstatement, an inner spiritual power potent enough to enable you to win the victory. So, when in the Far Country the Prodigal comes to himself and says, "I will arise and go to my father," there is not a vast indifference at the other end of the journey, but a father where deep can call unto deep.

Take a further step and note that life runs out into its depths not only in trouble, love, and moral need, but in the very opposite of moral need—profound sacrificial ethical devotion. Once Abraham Lincoln was taken to task by his friends for some criticism that his policies were evoking, and he said this to them: "I do the very best I know how—the very best I can; and I mean to keep doing so until the end. If the end brings me out all right, what is said against me won't amount to anything. If the end brings me out wrong, ten angels swearing I was right would make no difference." When a man thus honestly cares about doing right, when he is profoundly in earnest about setting his compass to the true pole, he wants to know that there is a true pole there to be true to. He cannot be content with subjective feeling only; he wants an objective right to be dedicated to. As Lincoln himself said on another occasion, "The question is not first of all whether God is on our side, but whether we are on God's side." When a man has sacrificial devotion to give, he wants a real God to give it to.

When Jesus in Gethsemane said, "Not my will, but thine, be done," that was a deep experience. But picture Jesus going into Gethsemane and finding there awaiting him nothing but what irreligion can offer—a vast indifference! How different his story would have been! When one has a great ethical devotion to give, he wants a great God to give it to.

Well, trouble, love, moral need, ethical devotion—such deeps are in us, and one other too, spiritual insight. As Browning said,

> Oh, we're sunk enough here, God knows!
> But not quite so sunk that moments,
> Sure tho' seldom, are denied us,
> When the spirit's true endowments
> Stand out plainly from its false ones.

We do have hours of insight like that, when the ground rises under our feet and the horizons expand and the vision grows clear. Who here does not understand such hours—under the spell of great music, under the stars at night, in the presence of high mountains, in quiet hours of receptive meditation, in crises when the soul rises up to make momentous choices—and how could one better sum up the witness of hours like that than by saying that when insight thus is clarified we see and feel the deep in us answered by a corresponding depth, and the best in us finding response in the Eternal Spirit?

So the Christian faith is fighting a battle for what we see and feel in our hours of deep trouble, deep love, deep moral need, deep ethical devotion, and profound spiritual insight. And if someone says, But life is not all such serious business, I say, No, but it is the deep sea that supports the dancing waves upon the surface; it is the profundities that sustain the super-ficialities and make them lovely; and if a man tries to live only in the shallows, with no deeps answering his deep, then the Nemesis is that some day his shallows will grow intolerably wearisome.

Note, now, the conclusion of the matter. Throughout this sermon we have been starting with the profundities in ourselves, and saying that they are answered by profundities in God. Suppose, however, that someone asks, What makes you think that these profundities in God that Christian faith believes in are really there? I would say in answer, Where did the profundities in ourselves come from? How did they get here? If fish have fins, it is because the water was there first. If birds have wings, it is because air was there first. If we have eyes, it is because the sun was there first. All the func-tions of living beings are but responses to something objec-tive in the universe. Always the universe was there first, and our powers and capacities are but our answer to it. How can one suppose that the deeps in the human spirit are the only exceptions to this universal law? In a world where lungs argue the priority of air, where eyes argue the priority of light, where the esthetic instincts in man argue the priority of beauty, where scientific curiosity in man argues the priority of truth, how can it be that the deepest things in man—great fortitude, great love, great moral want, great devotion, deep insight— argue the priority of *nothing*? It is preposterous.

So, in a sense, our whole sermon has been wrong side up. We started with profundity in man and saw it answered by profundity in God, but the deeper truth is that God came first, and all that is fine, true and beautiful in us is but our partial response to him. As the New Testament says, "We love him, because he first loved us." So today may the deep in the Eternal call unto the deep in us, and may there be indeed in our spirit a depth to answer it.

After Forty Years in the Ministry*

ORTY years ago this week I was ordained to the Christian ministry. This morning I speak to you about what seems to me the most important contrast between that older generation's attitude toward the Christian message and the attitude that challenges us now. To put it briefly, liberal Christians forty years ago were doing their best to adjust Christianity to modern science and modern civilization. It was science then and the civilization that science was producing that was standard, and Christianity had to be accommodated to and made conformable with that. Christianity, we said, is backward, set in outgrown ways of thinking, and we must bring it up to date, modernize it, and fit it into the fashions of thought and action for which science stands.

Today, far from denying, I would reaffirm, the necessity of that process. Christ himself told us to love the Lord our God with all our minds, and so inevitably do mental categories change and new formulations of knowledge come, that each generation must rethink its faith if its faith is to be real. Today, however, looking back over forty years of ministry, I see an outstanding difference between then and now with regard to what is standard and who must do the adjusting. What man in his senses can now call our modern civilization "standard"? It is not Christ's message that needs to be accommodated to this mad scene; it is this mad scene into which our civilization has collapsed that needs to be judged and saved by Christ's message. This is the most significant change distinguishing the beginning of my ministry from now. Then we were trying to accommodate Christ to our scientific civilization; now we

* Preached November 14, 1943.

face the desperate need of accommodating our scientific civilization to Christ.

The effect of this change is startling to one whose memories go back as far as mine. My own personal problem had been the rethinking of Christianity's message in modern terms so that it would be intelligible; and the early years of my ministry were engaged above all else in trying to make the Christian gospel intellectually palatable to modern minds that believed in such truths as evolution and the reign of natural law. That had to be done, but now, when it is done, when only belated minds suppose that Christianity must be thought of in pre-scientific terms, how radically the relationship between Christ and this modern scientific civilization has shifted! Who now needs to do the adjusting?

Will Durant has said, "The First World War did more harm to Christianity than all the Voltaires in history; the Second World War may complete its destruction." Certainly these two world wars have hurt Christianity terribly, but have they not hurt something else much more? They have desperately shaken our optimistic confidence in our modern scientific civilization. One sentence from an English newspaper sums it up: "Man has conquered the air only to be compelled to burrow under ground." Who now needs to do the adjusting—Christ to this civilization, or this civilization to Christ? For my anniversary text, therefore, I choose a verse from Paul's second letter to the Corinthians as Dr. Moffatt translates it: "It is no weak Christ you have to do with, but a Christ of power."

When we inquire why this shift has taken place, until Christ becomes the criterion by which we must test even our proud scientific culture, one answer at least is plain. Our intellectual formulations can never be an ultimate standard. Important as they are, they continually fluctuate and change, and are among the most inconstant, transient aspects of our lives. Intellectually we condescend even to the greatest characters of antiquity. A grammar school boy now knows infinitely more than Isaiah knew about the cosmos. Plato and Jeremiah, Paul and Jesus, Saint Augustine, Saint Francis, and all the rest—what outgrown, pre-scientific views they held! So, looking back, we see across the ages man's scientific information grow, and, picturing ourselves upon the pinnacle of progress, we pride ourselves on our superiority. But we forget that this process of information's growth has just begun, that each decade accelerates its speed so that a hundred years from now our posterity will be condescending to us, saying, What naïve and childish views they held, and how outgrown their intellectual formulations were! If, therefore, our intellectual formulations, important as they are, are thus partial, tentative, and transient —as Sir Isaac Newton said about himself, only picking up a few shells on the shores of this vast, unfathomable sea of our universe—they cannot be the solid test and final standard to which all else must be accommodated.

There is another realm, however, where we cannot condescend to the great seers of the past. Forty years ago we were saying, How can we adjust Christianity to the reign of natural law, to evolution, and all the rest? Today we think that easy; only belated minds are bothered by that now, and the real problem looms infinitely more difficult: How can we adjust our scientific civilization to the Golden Rule? How can we bring it to terms with Christ's idea of the sacredness of personality and with his principles of justice, goodwill, liberty, and brotherhood? These are the towering standards now, and our critical need is not Christianity's adjustment to our civilization but our civilization's adjustment to the basic principles of the Sermon on the Mount. "Whether there be knowledge," wrote Paul, "it shall vanish away. . . . But now abideth faith, hope, love, these three; and the greatest of these is love." Nothing ever written has been more confirmed by history than that. So it is a Christ of power we have to deal with, saying to our proud scientific world, You have tried accommodating me to your culture, and see where you have landed! Suppose now you try accommodating your culture to me!

As we seek to illustrate this and to apply it to ourselves, consider for one thing that it humbles our intellectual pride. Forty years ago we were intellectually very proud. Not only did we know more than ever had been known on earth before, but we were turning this knowledge to marvelous inventive purposes. I am not belittling this—the achievements of inventive science have been magnificent. But after all, inventive science is only a tool we use, with everything depending on the quality of spirit that uses it and the ethical ends for which it is employed. A recent writer pictures a man staring through the window of a power plant at the whirling dynamos there and thinking, "Man contrived to steal power from the gods, but, the fool he is, he forgot to bring with it the clue to its right use, and here is Chaos come again."

Forty years ago we did not feel that. Forty years ago did I say? In 1912 an eminent American professor said this: "To-day we have no fear of war, famine, pestilence, or failing resources. The advance of knowledge has safeguarded men from all those evils." How intellectually proud we were! And as for Christianity, multitudes were thinking that it must fit itself as best it could to our amazing new knowledge and to the triumphant progress of our ascending life. But now see what room is left for pride!

This shift of emphasis has changed the very location of Christ when we think of him. Forty years ago he was often thought of as an ancient character, a child of his times, a prisoner of his date, and as Christians we were anxious lest we should lose him back there in the far-off generation when he lived. So a poet of that day put it:

> Comes faint and far Thy voice
> From vales of Galilee;
> Thy vision fades in ancient shades;
> How should we follow Thee?

Today, however, far from being a dim figure back in history, Christ and his message are among the most vivid and urgent facts we face, so that this last week one of our leading industrialists said that if ever we get our industrial relations on a decent basis, it must be upon the principles that Christ laid down. How urgently contemporaneous Christ and his message are, saying to this ghastly and shaken world, If any man will hear these words of mine and will do them, I will liken him unto a wise man who built his house upon the rock!

Since this is an anniversary sermon, let me put it personally. The Revolutionary War ruined the Fosdick family. In 1700 Samuel Fosdick was one of the leading citizens of New London, Connecticut, so prosperous and happy that a contemporary chronicler writes, "A glance at the inventory of Captain Fosdick will show the ample and comfortable style of housekeeping to which the inhabitants had attained in 1700." So my family flourished until the Revolutionary War, but at its end we were ruined and penniless. It took two generations before the children in our household had a decent chance again. It was my grandfather who began to climb out, and he wrote, "As a family we struggled against poverty and ignorance."

Since the Revolutionary War the world has seen an incredible advance of scientific knowledge, and yet what happened to my family is happening now, on a scale never known before, to millions of families around the world, for whose offspring it will be generations before a decent chance comes back again. Obviously, knowledge alone cannot save us. Something else altogether is the abiding standard to whose arbitrament knowledge itself must be brought if it is not to ruin us. The eternal right—Christ, his faith, his basic principles, his character, his way of life—that is the standard. Let the church stop its apologetic tone and face its gigantic task, unworthy though it is to face it, for that task is not to adjust Christ to this modern civilization but to adjust this modern civilization to Christ!

Consider, further, that this truth humbles not only our

[205]

intellectual but our ethical pride. Forty years ago we proudly thought that we were not only growing wiser but morally better, too. Listen to Dr. Newell Dwight Hillis in a typical utterance of those days: "Laws are becoming more just, rulers humane; music is becoming sweeter and books wiser; homes are happier, and the individual heart becoming at once more just and more gentle." How ridiculous that sounds now! But then that was the prevalent, popular, optimistic mood, backed by the authority of great names like Herbert Spencer, who told us that progress toward an ever better world was an inevitable law.

In that mood we did a logical thing: taking our contemporary institutions—the nation, our business, our social sets, our schools and churches—and, believing that they were inevitably growing better, we tried to fit Christ into them as best we could. Nationalism, for example—proud, belligerent, imperialistic—we accepted that, only, of course, we wanted to fit Christ into it and so gradually improve it. Business, also —powerful, aggressive, conquering new areas, raising the standard of living, but often ruthless and predatory—we accepted that, only, of course, we wanted to mollify and ameliorate it by fitting Christ into it as best we could. So, with one social institution after another our adjustment of Christ to our civilization was not only intellectual but practical and ethical.

Look at the consequence! We made central and primary the self-interest of our nations, our business, our social sets, and our personal lives, and we put the eternal ethical standards into a secondary place. That was a fateful thing to do and now we face the logical result: Hitler, for example, saying that anything is right that helps the Nazi party, and anything wrong that hurts it—*that* the test and standard; Mussolini saying that anything is right that helps fascism—*that* the criterion. We shudder at such frank and brutal declarations—as Lenin bluntly put it, "We say that a morality taken from outside of human society does not exist for us; it is a fraud. For us morality is subordinated to the interests of the proletarian class-struggle." Yet we too have shared in such denial. It was not Hitler but an American who said that "Morality . . . is really nothing but a fashion, which changes from one year to another, from one country to another, from one place to another, and more especially from one person to another, as surely as the fashion and taste in hats or furniture." There is nothing, then, everlastingly right, greater than any nation, sovereign above all human relationships, to which we must adjust ourselves?

Such time as is left now for my ministry is dedicated to one major aim—to help put back again where it belongs the truth that there is an everlasting right to which our nations, our business, our racial relationships, our schools and churches and our personal lives must be conformed if any salvation is to visit us.

To be sure, there are moral customs that are like fashions in hats and furniture. On the road in England one passes to the left; here, we pass to the right—there are moral customs like that, matters of convention that change from place to place. But this fact does not begin to cover the ground. Nothing can make Judas Iscariot right—nothing! Everywhere and always he is wrong. To do to others what we would not have them do to us—nothing anywhere at any time can make that right. Vindictive hatred, cruelty, the misuse of power that hurts others—nothing can ever make that right. To trample on the souls of men and violate their inherent liberty—that is not a matter of fashion to be determined by our self-interest but is eternally wrong. There is a standard right—the moral law of God built into the structure of this universe—to which we and all our institutions must subject ourselves or else be lost; and when we wish to see that law supremely incarnate and exhibited, there is none other to compare with Christ. Ah, Paul, you were talking about us, too! It is no weak Christ you have to deal with but a Christ of power.

This world war is ruining many reputations. It is certainly ruining the reputation of war itself, that many have praised as a spur to progress. Who can call war a spur to progress now? This conflict is ruining the reputation of isolated, irresponsible nationalism; and even our pride in inventive science, with which we desolate the world, this war is deeply humiliating. It is hurting terribly the reputation of the Christian church that after nearly two thousand years leaves Europe, where it has had its longest chance, the plague spot of the world. But among all the ruined reputations one reputation rises more impressive and imperious than ever—the Christ of the Sermon on the Mount, the Christ of the eternally right, to whom we and our institutions must adjust ourselves or fall from one catastrophe to another. He shines undimmed, like a beacon at the harbor's mouth where our peace lies. Put the Kingdom of God first, he said, and there is some hope that the social blessings we desire may be added unto us. Is not that realistically true? Put the Kingdom of God first, and there is hope that our economic inequity and strife may be resolved, and all the people find open doors to prosperity and happiness. Put God's sovereignty first in racial relationships, and the awful spectre of war between the white and colored races may be replaced by understanding and goodwill. The word of the Master is eternally true—all the homely, decent, ordinary, day by day things we want most depend on our putting Christ's way of life first.

If that is true about social relationships, it is surely true about us one by one. There are some things that we must adjust ourselves to. The universe with its eternal laws was here first—we must adjust ourselves to that. Christ, the revelation of the everlasting right, antedates us, overarches us; Alpha and Omega, he was here first and will be here last—not ours to use and fit into our ways but ours to follow and obey.

> O Lord and Master of us all,
>   Whate'er our name or sign,
> We own thy sway, we hear thy call,
>   We test our lives by thine.

The Light That No Darkness Can Put Out*

WHEN the stories about Jesus' birth took form in the early church they emphasized the fact that it was night when he was born. The shepherds were keeping watch over their flocks by night; the wise men were following the star through the night; in Herod's gloomy midnight councils all the little children of Bethlehem were to be slain, and every way it was against encompassing darkness that Christ's coming shone out.

When people now say that these are dour times in which to keep Christmas, they forget this basic fact about the Christmas stories. This is indeed a dark time, but if what those first narratives say in symbol and what Phillips Brooks long afterward sang of Bethlehem is true,

> Yet in thy dark streets shineth
> The everlasting Light,

then all the more this is a grand era in which to understand what Christmas really means. In easier times we left the night out of the picture and made of the Christmas season a light-hearted holiday of festival and merriment, but now we are back where Christmas started—with its deep, black background behind the Savior's coming, like midnight behind the star.

Nearly a hundred years after Bethlehem the writer of the Fourth Gospel was still thinking of Christ's advent in terms of light shining in darkness. John, too, lived in a dour world, in Ephesus, where the goddess Diana was worshiped under the image of a meteorite stone, and in an age shadowed by paganism and violence. Yet something had happened to him

* A Christmas sermon.

that, as Clement of Alexandria later put it, had "changed sunset into sunrise." Christ had come, and all through his Gospel, John speaks of him in terms of light. "In him," John writes in his first chapter, "was life; and the life was the light of men . . . the light shineth in the darkness; and the darkness apprehended it not." That last phrase is a mistranslation; scholars would now substantially agree, I think, with Dr. Goodspeed's better rendering: "The light is still shining in the darkness, for the darkness has never put it out." That fact John proclaims with amazement and gratitude—the night so black, the radiance of Christ at first so limited, he stands in awe before the fact that after nearly a century the light is still shining.

Surely, that is a Christmas text for us now. Not after one century, but after nearly twenty, we still can say at least this much about the radiance Christ kindled in the world: The darkness has not put it out.

Note at once the contrast between John and ourselves with regard to the place where the emphasis is put. We are tempted to be obsessed by the darkness. This is a gloomy time, we say. John, upon the contrary, takes the darkness for granted. Of course, darkness! What kind of world do you think this is, he would say to us; stop fooling yourselves with sentimental optimism; the sin of the world is beastly; the plight of the world desperate; man's moral depravity and incompetence profound—of course, darkness! So John took the world's black night for granted, and with amazement and gratitude emphasized the light. *There* to him was the astonishing fact, that against the night a guiding star had shined, that into the gloom a flaming hope had come, and that all the hosts of evil had been unable to quench it.

As we translate this way of looking at Christ's coming into the terms of our experience now, consider first that it presents us with a great heritage—the continuing influence of Christ— to which we ought to give our personal faith and allegiance.

There can be no wiser counsel in a dark time than to get our eyes on whatever light there is in our heritage, believe in that and follow it. A friend of mine was once lost in the woods in the Adirondacks, and as night came on, completely bewildered, he climbed a tree, and there, far off and dim, he saw a single light. It was not much, but it was something to center his faith on, and guide his steps by, in the night. Well, in our heritage there is a great light that the darkness has never been able to put out.

This is true in our national life. When I for one think of these years ahead, when the use we make of America's predominant power will have such fateful consequence for the world's future, I am more anxious about this nation than ever before in my life. So Lord Milner said once, "The last thing which the thought of the [British] Empire inspires in me is a desire to boast—to wave a flag, or to shout 'Rule Britannia.' When I think of it, I am much more inclined to go into a corner by myself and pray." So we had better pray for America now, that the best in our national heritage—the light there —may be seen and followed. For with all our materialism, our greed, our selfish nationalism and isolationism, there is, in our American tradition at its best, a light—men and women to whom America's power has been a sacred trust to be used in the sight of God for the good of all mankind. Remember John Adams, a founding father, saying, "I always consider the settlement of America with reverence and wonder, as the opening of a grand scene and design in Providence for the illumination of the ignorant, and the emancipation of the slavish part of mankind all over the earth." God grant now that we may believe in that best of our tradition! As for us Christians, what a heritage we have! Illumination did come to the world in Christ, and amid the blackness of our Western history his radiance has spread, in every generation some men and women rediscovering him and his way of life and so producing the noblest character that shines amid history's cruelty and gloom; and the most amazing fact about it is that all the hosts of darkness have never been able to put it out.

They have tried hard enough. From Herod's bloody plot to slay Bethlehem's children, to Caiaphas and Pilate, the Gospels portray the mad endeavors of dark powers to put out that flame of life and hope. In *Othello* you recall the fateful hour when the jealous Moor comes into Desdemona's room to slay her, and, extinguishing the candle, says, "Put out the light, and then put out the light." So, more than once in the Gospels and in subsequent history one stands, as it were, with bated breath as the powers of evil seem about to quench the flame that was kindled at Bethlehem.

About thirty-five years after Calvary the Roman historian Tacitus wrote in astonishment and indignation because the Christian movement had gone on so long unstopped: This "pestilent superstition," Tacitus wrote, "though checked for the time being, broke out afresh, not only in Judea, where the mischief started, but also at Rome, where all manner of horrible and loathsome things pour in and become fashionable." So, from the first, to a scholar like Tacitus it seemed incredible that the flame Christ kindled should go on burning. Here is the marvel of history, not that the world is dark —it always has been—but that we have a radiant spiritual heritage, coming down to us across the centuries, that all the hosts of evil have not been able to quench.

In this congregation this Christmas Sunday I want some personal decisions made, some serious self-committals here. In our world now antichrist does loom, dark and terrifying. Take a good look at him—antichrist incarnate and black as midnight! Some things are being done on earth this Christmastime so hideous that the mind recoils, seared and blistered with shame, and turbulent with indignation. All the more shall we not say, Still in the darkness the light shineth—in *that* I will believe? Christ never seemed to me so important as now when antichrist is so black. A friend once asked

William Howard Taft what he thought about the League of Nations, and he answered, "Well, the best things of life get crucified and put in a tomb. But they always have their third day." That is a creed for Christians now. To be sure, darkness! To be sure, crucifixion and the tomb! But still the light that the darkness never can put out—in that I believe.

Consider again that not only does this truth present to our faith a great heritage of spiritual illumination, but it presents a supreme personality in whom the victory of light over darkness was actually consummated. The New Testament keeps coming back to that. It was dreadfully difficult then to believe that Christ's way of life could rise triumphant over the world's evil, but still, in one place that actually had happened. Christ himself presented an achieved victory—not simply an ideal, not merely an argument, but a fact, a resplendent, undeniable triumph of sunrise over night. So John pictures Jesus himself saying, "In the world ye have tribulation: but be of good cheer; I have overcome the world."

As Gladstone said, "One example is worth a thousand arguments." In every realm the final proof is commonly reached not by debate but by achievement. It cannot be done, men say of some things seemingly incredible, as only forty years ago they were saying about aviation; and they keep on saying it, theoretically arguing with persuasive plausibility that it cannot be done. And then it is done. That is the answer. How many arguments in human history have been suddenly stopped not by opposing arguments but by a shining fact: It has been done.

So this light we are talking of at Christmastime is a fact, personally consummated in a life. On a priori grounds a life like Christ's, the Sermon on the Mount incarnate in a man who was crucified and yet who has gone on and on, the most potent spiritual influence that ever came to earth, is utterly incredible. No argument could ever have made it plausible. To tell the tale in advance of its happening, a man born in a manger, dying on a cross, distinguished only by love and humility, who shakes the world to its foundations and two thousand years afterwards is the criterion by whom millions test the characters of men and the policies of nations—that is the wildest impossibility that could be presented to the minds of men. But the argument against that has long since been stopped. That has been done.

How realistically true in many realms this fact is of which we now are speaking! You cannot educate the masses, men once argued; only the privileged classes produce minds that are worth educating; the masses of the people must be left as they are—illiterate hewers of wood and drawers of water. So they argued, and they were never finally answered by opposing arguments. How could they be? They were answered by lives, like Faraday, underprivileged, coming up out of unpromising circumstances, and yet becoming one of the most creative scientists of his time. So, our modern democracies have opened wide the doors of education to everybody, persuaded not by debate but by example that we can never tell where the great minds are coming from.

Here lies the ultimate solution of the Negro problem. The Negro is essentially an inferior race, men have argued; racial equality is absurd; Negroes have no place except in menial tasks, and can never rise to take their place beside the white man. So the argument has run, and no opposing argument can ever answer it. But then Marian Anderson sings, George Washington Carver becomes one of our greatest American scientists, a Negro girl at Yale wins first prize in the annual competition of young American poets, a New York Negro tops the list of citations for meritorious police duty, a new Liberty ship named the "Booker T. Washington," christened by a Negro woman, sails the seas with a crew of white and black commanded by a Negro captain. That is the answer. Always the arguments of skeptics run on and on until they fade out in the light of fact.

All such illustrations are small and partial examples of something everlastingly true that makes Christmas forever worth celebrating. This is a dark world, men think. I should say it is! But something else is really here—a new kind of life that did come into the world in Christ, and that, as John said, is the "light of men." No longer a matter of theoretical argument, that is an achieved victory, an accomplished fact. If anyone says now that light cannot conquer darkness, the answer is, it has been done. To which, then, are we giving our faith and allegiance—to the night or to the sunrise?

Come a step further now and see what immense encouragement this truth brings. The other evening some of us heard one of the missionaries who came back on the "Gripsholm" say that when she was taken from her work in Japan, to which she had given the best years of her life, and was sent to a concentration camp, one sentence summed up her hope and reinforced her courage: "All the darkness in the world," she kept repeating to herself, "cannot put out the light of a single candle." So!

In a familiar hymn we sing our thankfulness that

> In the darkest spot of earth
> Some love is found.

That is true. In Germany now there is a concentration camp where British prisoners are kept—a dark place where none of us would wish to be—but there today is a British medical officer, an ophthalmic surgeon, who could have been exchanged and sent home. He was on the list to go back to England and he refused. Everybody, even the Germans, expostulated with him. He had every right to go home, but he said this: "While I have been here in this prison camp I have been able to treat blinded prisoners, and in some cases to restore their sight. Others, in similar need, will come to this camp and I want to remain to help them." In what darkest spot on earth is not some light to be found? Moreover, something deep in every one of us responds to John's faith—it is the light that will last; the darkness will never put it out.

To be sure, there is a stern aspect to light. It is not simply beautiful; it shows things up. Sometimes when light shines it is terrific. This boy, with soiled face and hands, who does not wish to cleanse himself, would be glad to have his mother look at him in the dark—he can get by there—but in the light she will see the truth about him. Light is not simply lovely; it is a judge, falling in silent condemnation on the things that it shows up. So John put it, "This is the judgment, that the light is come into the world, and men loved the darkness rather than the light; for their works were evil."

Stern though this truth is, however, our hope is there. We would never know that anything is crooked if we had never seen anything straight. We would never know that anything is evil if we had never seen anything good. We would never even know that it is dark if light had not come. Take a lovely home this Christmastime, radiant with the fairest meanings that family life can know, and put it beside an embittered home, harsh with discord and distrust, and it is the lovely home that shows the bad home up. We would never know how bad a bad home is if we had never seen how beautiful a good home can be. In every realm this is the judgment, that light has come into the world.

Granted, the stern aspects of this truth, yet it is our hope, for when lovely homes have once appeared there is something in mankind that cannot escape taking them as standard. They become the criterion by whose arbitrament we judge all other homes, and we are unhappily dissatisfied when we fail that test. When Christlike character has once appeared, creatively beautiful with humility, humaneness, and goodwill, despite ourselves and all our evil that kind of character moves up into the central place and becomes the judgment seat where other character is tried. Yes, when once the world catches a glimpse of itself organized for peace instead of war, something happens that all the forces of darkness cannot prevent: that vision becomes the standard of our judgment, the criterion of our endeavor, and short of it mankind will never be content. So John was not dreaming. He was dealing with everlasting fact. When light comes it stays; it shows up evil; it becomes the test and criterion of hope and of endeavor; and not all the darkness in the world can put out the light of a single candle when once it has been lighted.

This has been the faith of those strong souls whose wisdom and sacrifice have won for us whatever good we have achieved on earth. Lord Shaftesbury is typical, writing in his diary after a hard fight in Parliament for a bill to improve the condition of the poor: "I was defeated last night—cast down but not destroyed. The stillest, darkest hour is just before the dawn. Righteousness will prevail." So may we keep Christmas in our hearts this year! The light is still shining in the darkness, and the darkness can never put it out.

Facing Life's Central Test*

MATTHEW'S Gospel tells us that in the Garden of Gethsemane Jesus fell on his knees and prayed, "O my Father, if it be possible, let this cup pass from me: nevertheless. . . ." We know what followed that crucial word: "Nevertheless not as I will, but as thou wilt." But reading the passage lately my thought stopped with that powerful conjunction and dwelt on its immense significance. "If it be possible, let this cup pass from me: nevertheless. . . ."

The first part of that text describes the situation of every one of us. Each heart here is praying to be spared, if possible, some tragedy so real to imagination that with many of us day and night the thought of it is in our minds. Soldiers going to the front, not wanting to be maimed or slain; others left at home, caring for these absent ones and their families with endless solicitude and affection—all of us today are praying, "O my Father, if it be possible, let this cup pass from me." And the central test of our lives now is whether we can take that next step—"Nevertheless."

Set in such a context, that word is one of the most momentous in the vocabulary and it brings Gethsemane close to all of us. To be sure, Jesus' struggle in the garden was unique, and this Holy Week, watching him move from the popularity of the shouting crowds on Palm Sunday to the loneliness of his agony underneath the trees, we look with awe upon its sacred mystery. But in another sense Gethsemane pictures the problem of every life. To face for conscience' sake the doing of a duty likely to cost us dear, to confront a handicap that cripples life or a tragedy that desolates it, saying, "If it be

* A Palm Sunday sermon.

possible, let this cup pass . . . nevertheless"—at that place a man proves how much of a man he is, and in these days none of us escapes the test. Charles Kingsley, preaching in his little village church at Eversley, used to lean over the pulpit on Sunday morning and say, "Here we are again to talk about what is really going on in your soul and mine." Well, this certainly is going on in our souls, this deep desire to be spared, if possible, something that we dread—with the question rising whether we can finish that prayer, as though to say, Though our private petition be denied, though duty cost dearly, and handicap and tragedy befall, nonetheless we will not crumple up and give in but will keep faith and carry on.

Unforgettable in the fascinated memory of man are the souls who have met that test. The Jews still celebrate at the festival of Purim the time when long ago Esther, the queen, met it. With everything to live for, with no need save her own conscience to identify herself with her stricken people, taking her life in her hands, she went up from her Gethsemane to present to the king her dangerous petition, saying, "If I perish, I perish." Esther is reduplicated many times in these days. It was an American airman who wrote:

Almighty and all present Power,
Short is the prayer I make to Thee,
I do not ask in battle hour
For any shield to cover me.

The vast unalterable way,
From which the stars do not depart
May not be turned aside to stay
The bullet flying to my heart.

But this I pray, be at my side
When death is drawing through the sky.
Almighty God who also died
Teach me the way that I should die.

So! "If it be possible, . . . nevertheless. . . ."

For one thing, in the way we meet this kind of situation lies the test of our faith in God. It is not difficult to have faith in God on our Palm Sundays, when everything seems to be coming our way, when the crowds shout approval, and life, as it were, strews palm branches in our path. Almost anyone can believe in God then. But when life passes from Palm Sunday to Gethsemane, with dangerous duty looming, with a possible cross ahead, and with the heart crying, Let this cup pass!— then the test comes, whether our faith in God is of a kind fitted not simply for fair weather but for foul.

The Book of Daniel tells the story of Nebuchadnezzar, the king, who made a golden image, requiring that when the music sounded all should fall down and worship it. Shadrach, Meshach, and Abednego refused, and Nebuchadnezzar threatened them with the burning fiery furnace. That was their Gethsemane, and we read: "Shadrach, Meshach, and Abednego answered and said to the king, O Nebuchadnezzar, we have no need to answer thee in this matter. If it be so, our God whom we serve is able to deliver us from the burning fiery furnace; and he will deliver us out of thy hand, O king. But if not, be it known unto thee, O king, that we will not serve thy gods, nor worship the golden image which thou hast set up." At that point does come the crucial test of our faith in God. He is able to deliver us; he will deliver us; *but if not* —my soul, what faith it takes to go on from there!

Surely this raises a personal question in every life here. What kind of faith in God have we with which to meet what confronts us now—fair weather faith that only amid the flowers of Galilee or the applauding crowds of Palm Sunday can believe in him? That was not enough for Christ, nor is it enough for any life today.

There are two kinds of faith in God. One says *if*—if all goes well, if life is hopeful, prosperous and happy, then I will believe in God; the other says *though*—though the forces of evil triumph, though everything goes wrong and Gethsemane comes and the cross looms, nevertheless, I will believe in God. The Bible is full of this contrast. On the one side is Jacob, saying, "If God will be with me, and will keep me in this way that I go, and will give me bread to eat, and raiment to put on, so that I come again to my father's house in peace, then shall the Lord be my God." That is fair weather faith, bargaining with God to trust him if all goes well, and in any Gethsemane it collapses. But listen to this other kind of faith, beginning not with "if" but with "though": "Though he slay me, yet will I trust in him"; "Though I walk through the valley of the shadow of death, I will fear no evil: for thou art with me"; "Though the waters thereof roar and be troubled, though the mountains shake with the swelling thereof. . . . The Lord of hosts is with us; the God of Jacob is our refuge."

You see, not on Palm Sunday with its hosannas, but in Gethsemane the real test comes, and there, at the very point where fair weather faith goes to pieces, the supreme rememberable faith of great souls rises to its height. It is going to take such faith to see us through these days. "If it be possible, let this cup pass from me: nevertheless. . . ."

Consider further that here lies the test not only of our faith in God but of our personal character. We never quite find out what kind of persons we are on our Palm Sundays; it is in Gethsemane we discover how much character we have.

Who of us cannot think, as I do now, of some special person in his Gethsemane today? He and his friends have prayed that this cup might pass from him, but it is not to be. He is drinking that cup now, and as the shadows encompass the hopes that he and his friends have prayed might be fulfilled, a strange triumph lights up his room like that which illumined even the darkness of Gethsemane. We always knew that he had character but now a depth is in it, and, as it were, a halo over it never seen before, for he is in the place where character is most severely tested and most impressively revealed and he is meeting it superbly. As it takes the night to reveal the stars, so it takes Gethsemane to reveal character like that. No one in the end escapes that test. When we have prayed, "Let this cup pass," and now see that it cannot pass, are there resources deep within us from which will rise that further word, that those who hear it never can forget?

One of the paradoxes of history is the influence which such characters have wielded on the world. In a sense Palm Sunday represents success, and Gethsemane, failure. On Palm Sunday the crowds are with us; the world seems moving our way; hosannas fill the air; palm branches line the road. In Gethsemane our hopes are dashed, our prayers denied; the forces of evil seem to triumph and sometimes we verily sweat blood. Yet, out of the world's Gethsemanes have come the characters that most of all we find it impossible to forget.

Captain Scott, for example, dying in the Antarctic. He did not reach the South Pole first—Amundsen beat him; he did not get back; his prayer was not answered; he failed. So what? So a few sentences that the world will never forget: "I do not regret this journey. . . . We took risks; we knew we took them; things have come out against us, and therefore we have no cause for complaint, but bow to the will of Providence, determined still to do our best to the last." So! "If it be possible, . . . nevertheless. . . ."

Here is a mystery in human life—the amazing success of failure. For in a sense, as the world saw it, Christ was a failure. Every time Holy Week comes round the amazing fact confronts us again, that we are celebrating a failure—a great soul whose family did not understand him, whose nation rejected him, whose government crucified him, whose hopes were dashed and whose prayers denied until on Calvary he cried, "My God, my God, why hast thou forsaken me?" What paradox can equal this: that nearly two thousand years afterward, with awe and reverence inexpressible, we celebrate so great a failure? Here is a mystery, that in a situation so dismaying character can rise to such heights and take such hold upon our race that when the so-called successes of millenniums have come and gone, men still will be remembering him who in a desperate time when all seemed lost said, "Nevertheless."

Come further now and see that here lies the test not only of our faith and character, but of our loyalty, our devotion to something greater than ourselves. After all, that word "nevertheless" is explained by what comes after it: "Not as I will, but as thou wilt." Jesus belonged to something—to the will of God. He was more than himself—himself plus what he had given himself to and stood for, on behalf of which he was willing to die. Only when a man has that element in his life can he, in the last ditch, behave at all like the Master in Gethsemane.

At this point we Americans in general and we Christians in particular face now a terrific competition. Many among us are still talking primarily about our rights. All praise to those who with unstinted loyalty and sacrifice are giving their lives for conscience' sake today, but still the fact remains that even in wartime and certainly in peacetime multitudes think of democracy in terms of the rights it gives them. Well, rights are important and our Bill of Rights is well worth celebrating. But one is given serious pause when one reads in the official organ of the Nazi Storm Troopers for May 14, 1942, this sentence: "Henceforth nobody has rights and everybody has only duties." If ever democracy forgets to balance rights with duties, it is indeed in danger when it confronts a social order that thus foregoes rights and exalts duties. The other day in one of our schools a youth, rebuked for flagrant disregard of social order, retorted: "But this is a public school, where I can do as I please." That is too common an idea of democracy—a social order where we can do as we please. Far from being so achieved in the first place, however, democracy was won by men who dedicated to it their lives, their fortunes, their sacred honor; nor will it be otherwise maintained. Believe me, our Bill of Rights needs to be balanced by a Bill of Duties! Especially now, immense issues are at stake—in the war, and in the peace that will follow it—issues so much more important than my individual good fortune or yours, that, taking the measure of them, one finds the best in him rising up to say about his merely personal desires to escape hardship, "If it be possible, . . . nevertheless. . . ."

William James of Harvard said once: "The difference between a good man and a bad one is the choice of the cause." What do we belong to so loyally that though everything goes wrong, and the cross looms and the triumph of what we believe in and want seems indefinitely postponed, still we do not give in? In our democracies now we need that spirit—a powerful swing of emphasis to balance rights with duties, and never more so than after the war is won. Then we shall confront duties—immense, world-wide in their significance—upon whose recognition and discharge the future of humanity for centuries depends.

As for our more intimate and private lives, a man sometime since committed suicide and left this note behind him: "A man has to be made of steel to endure nowadays." No, my friend, a man does not need to be made of steel, but he does need to be made of loyalty, of devotion to great aims that overpass his private interests, of allegiance to the will of God for the world our children will have to live in, allegiance so real that that prayer in Gethsemane will rise as the natural expression of the kind of person he genuinely is: "Nevertheless not as I will, but as thou wilt."

Where this truth applies most cogently to your life and mine, each heart must know from inside information, but it surely does apply. Off one of our Coast Guard stations in a tremendous storm with an offshore gale, a ship was wrecked on a reef. The captain ordered the lifeboat launched, but one of the crew protested. "Sir," he said, "the wind is offshore and the tide is running out. Of course we can go out, but what good will it do? Against the wind and the tide we cannot come back." "Launch the boat," said the captain. "We have to go out. We don't have to come back." Too many people are living in that spirit now for us to evade the application of it to ourselves. I know the prayers that rise from this congregation to be spared tragedy. In whose heart do not such prayers rise at times with inward agony? God grant that we may be spared—Jesus prayed that. *But if not*— At that point our discipleship to Jesus meets its test.

Once more we stand, then, at the beginning of another Holy Week and find ourselves part and parcel of the scene. We have had our Palm Sundays, when the air was filled with hosannas and all was well, but now our lives have moved out to a Gethsemane that takes the whole world in. It is terrific. It is a test of our faith, our character, our loyalty. But as nearly two millenniums afterward we keep the anniversary of one who met that test, let us remember that the whole world is always lifted when men meet it well.

An old Hindu quatrain runs thus:

> Like one who doubts an elephant
> When seeing him pass by,
> And yet believes when he has seen
> The footprints left, so I.

Well, had I been at Calvary I think I should have doubted. How futile that sacrifice, how final the failure! But now one sees the footprints left—Pilate gone, Caiaphas gone, empire after empire perished, and the world still turning to one who took upon himself a burden he did not need to take, who kept on loving when he was hated, who died for men when they did not deserve it, and who so let loose in the world the mightiest lifting force that ever gripped our race—vicarious self-sacrifice backed by a faith, a character, a loyalty that, though the heavens fell, would not give in. Ah, my soul, even afar off, follow him if you can! "If it be possible, let this cup pass from me; nevertheless. . . ."

The Deathless Hope That Man Cannot Escape*

EVERYONE here must be aware that this is more than just another Easter morning. Whatever else these years of war do, they advertise the fact of death; in tones too stentorian to be avoided they tell us that we must somehow come to terms with that.

To be sure, the Easter faith itself is old and the text we choose long familiar: "This corruptible must put on incorruption, and this mortal must put on immortality. So when this corruptible shall have put on incorruption, and this mortal shall have put on immortality, then shall be brought to pass the saying that is written, Death is swallowed up in victory." But while such faith is old, who does not feel an added poignancy, a special directness of personal appeal, on this Easter morning in the midst of war? Who here is not wondering whether he really has faith and spiritual resource enough to come to victorious terms, either with his own death or someone else's?

One of our most popular dramatic critics in this city some years ago published his creed, one item of which was this: "Never allow one's self even a passing thought of death." One wonders how he is getting on with that item now. Does he read the papers and not allow himself even a passing thought of death? To be sure, in one sense death is still a highly individual experience. As another put it, "Death is not like a factory gate through which men pass in throngs, but like a turnstile, through which men go one by one." Nevertheless, in war men are massed for death in multitudes; they storm it by battalions and regiments, so that today with poignant vividness we face its large-scale familiarity.

* An Easter sermon.

[226]

Moreover, not only is the fact of death made vivid this wartime Easter, but the interpretation of it—the question whether death is a period that brings the sentence of life to a full stop, or only a comma that punctuates it to a loftier significance—is made specially important. Some years ago one skeptical writer said that in our unwillingness to die and have that the end of us, we were no better than a lot of peevish children, who, having played outdoors all day, were unwilling to come in at eventide. Is that all there is to the question of death—to play outdoors all day and be willing to come in at eventide? These millions of youths around the world, now drafted into the armies of the nations and going out to the battlefields—have they played outdoors all day? Such flippancy about death's meaning is cheap enough at any time, but certainly it will not do now.

The most characteristic influence, however, that war brings to bear upon our Easter message is probably not the new vividness of the fact of death, nor the new personal importance of its meaning, but the discovery that when we human beings are shaken down into our depths we really do believe in life after death. Major Gordon, better known to us as Ralph Connor, came back from the last war, after two years in the trenches, saying that in all that time he had never met a man who did not believe in immortality. That is strange. In war when death comes it is stark naked. It cannot be concealed by the decent amenities that in civilized society our sensitive nerves devise. In war, death can neither be run away from nor covered up, and sometimes, day and night, one's senses are smitten by physical dissolution and decay. Yet it is precisely there, where man seems most mortal, that many to their own amazement find that when they are shaken down into their depths, the soul's invincible surmise is strong within them that somehow life goes on. So a Canadian soldier in the last war, seeing his chum blown to pieces by an exploding shell, said, "He'll carry on. It will take more than that to stop him."

This fact lights up a profound truth about all of us human beings. We sometimes picture ourselves as trying hard to believe in immortality. No! So far as we modern-minded folk are concerned, we might better be pictured as trying hard not to believe in it, constructing laborious arguments against it and elaborating our skepticisms to disprove it. Multitudes of us have tried not to believe in immortality—is it not one of the most incredible of faiths? But lo, some earthquake, as it were, shakes us down into our spiritual depths, and there it is again, that deathless hope that man cannot escape, that strange conviction that each of us is like a river, and that, though turning a bend called death we cannot see a rod beyond, the river still flows on.

That fact may well give to this Easter Day a special quality. We have no more arguments for immortality than we had before, but now life is shaking us down into our profounder levels, and the more that happens, the more our elaborate skepticisms about life eternal seem artificial and sophisticated; they are on the surface of our minds; we make them up out of our wits; but at the center of our life abides that strange, invincible surmise: "This corruptible must put on incorruption, and this mortal must put on immortality."

Why is this? Whence comes this deathless hope that man cannot escape?

For one thing, it comes from the way that we ourselves are made. The properties of which our bodies are constituted are one with sticks and stones and animals. For while we call our bodies temples "of the Holy Spirit," the material of which they are constructed has been dug from the common quarries of the earth, and when the body dies it is as natural as when leaves wither, or trees, blown from their rootage, are toppled over in a storm.

But it is not so with the realm of mind and spirit. Even now mind and spirit have essentially a timeless, limitless, eternal quality. There are no natural boundaries to the experience of love and beauty so that a man may think he has reached their consummation, but when his body ends, still, immeasurable miles beyond him, their possibilities beckon the spirit on. There are no natural limits to truth, that a man may comprehensively lay his hands upon it, for while the body falls on sleep as naturally as a child at night, the mind, like Goethe on his deathbed, still cries, "More light, more light!" There are no natural limits to character so that a man may reach its summit, for when he is at his best, lo, far above him Christ is standing, and were he to climb to Christ, even he would be looking upward, saying, "Why callest thou me good? none is good save one, even God." Thus the essential property of mind and spirit even here and now is that they dwell in realms timeless and limitless. Thus von Humboldt the scientist, nearly a century old, talking of a new clue to truth he had discovered, cried, "Oh, for another one hundred years!" So Corot, at seventy-seven, said, "If the Lord lets me live two years longer I think I can paint something beautiful." And so even we ordinary folk in our profounder hours find there something prophetic of more than earth can be the stage for, from which rises, almost despite ourselves, this powerful intimation of immortality.

Some try to dull the force of this by saying that mind and spirit are dependent on the body and therefore must perish when the body dies. But still the question rises, what do we mean, dependent on the body? The chick is dependent on the egg, absolutely dependent, but it is a temporary dependence in preparation for a future independence. The butterfly is dependent on the cocoon, absolutely dependent, but it is a temporary dependence in preparation for a future liberty. The unborn babe is absolutely dependent on the womb, but it is a dependence initial and preparatory, not final. Why may not the spirit of man be, to as great an extent as one may wish to phrase it, absolutely dependent on the body, but the dependence still be temporary, in preparation for a future freedom?

A man who has lived on earth seventy years has had ten bodies, has sloughed them off and lived on through them, and the strand of unity that makes his life still an identity, with one body after another strung upon it, is not simply physical. It is spiritual, self-conscious personality that sloughs off bodies and still lives on. That is the real mystery, and it is present here and now. Well, many of us do try not so much to believe in immortality as to disbelieve it, constructing many an argument against it, but then some great hour comes, and lo, there it is again, that inescapable intuition that within ourselves there is something that death has no dominion over!

Recall how one of Thornton Wilder's characters puts it in the play *Our Town*: "I don't care what they say with their mouths—everybody knows that *something* is eternal. And it ain't houses and it ain't names, and it ain't earth, and it ain't even stars . . . everybody knows in their bones that *something* is eternal, and that something has to do with human beings. All the greatest people ever lived have been telling us that for five thousand years and yet you'd be surprised how people are always losing hold of it. There's something way down deep that's eternal about every human being."

For still another reason when life shakes us down into our depths we find there this deathless hope, and that is our love for other people. We may grow nonchalant about life after death so far as we ourselves are concerned. Surely Goethe is right when he says, "An able man, who has something regular to do here, and must toil and struggle and produce day by day, leaves the future world to itself, and is active and useful in this." Right! No man in his normal senses thinks habitually about death and its aftermath. Nevertheless, that is not the whole story. Some day the bell tolls for someone's passing who is to us the very center and essence of life's meaning, and there it is once more, that deathless hope, like an artesian well, that our superficial forgetfulness may temporarily conceal but that in all great hours comes pouring up again.

Sometimes this experience is very intimate. A distinguished and beautiful person died some time ago, and the one who loved her better than he loved himself summed up one of the deepest cries of the human heart when he said, "God must not let anything happen to her." The one who said that was a very modern man; it would not have been surprising had he been skeptical about immortality; but in that hour when life went down into its depths, there it was once more, that deathless hope.

Sometimes this experience is more general, as though from some high hilltop one surveyed the amazing spectacle of evolution and saw the long and costly course by which personality has at last arrived. It is an astounding picture, this creation moving up from low to higher forms, from stardust to stellar universes, and on the earth, from inorganic to organic, from crystal to vegetable and animal, from animal to human, until the consummation of it comes in personality, its face lifted from the ground, daring to call God "Father" and aspire to be like him. Now, unless this creative process is utterly purposeless, something worth while and abiding must come of personality. Nothing else here lasts. The earth itself will have its uninhabitable ending when all life will perish on it. If anything is to come of this creative process, something must come of personality, and all our deepest hours rebel against thinking that nothing will come of it, that every personal soul will run into a blind alley and stop, until on a dying planet the whole race will run into a blind alley and stop, and the Creator, having wrought personality by the agony of a million million years, will toss it all away as a mere inadvertence, a caprice and whim. Darwin himself said he could not believe that.

Recall how Edna St. Vincent Millay puts it:

I am not resigned to the shutting away of loving hearts in
   the hard ground.
So it is, and so it will be, for so it has been, time out of mind:
Into the darkness they go, the wise and the lovely. Crowned
With lilies and with laurel they go; but I am not resigned.

. . . .

Down, down, down into the darkness of the grave
Gently they go, the beautiful, the tender, the kind;
Quietly they go, the intelligent, the witty, the brave.
I know. But I do not approve. And I am not resigned.

There speaks the human soul in its deepest hours.

And sometimes this experience has chiefly to do not so
much with intimate love or with general outlooks on personality's meaning and value, but with the great souls of the race,
the supreme spirits through whom a light divine has shined
upon the earth. They ought not to die and have that the end
of them. Go down to the North River, here in New York;
cannot a man tell the difference between a ferryboat and a
seagoing ship? Ferryboats look like ferryboats—we know
they could not make an ocean trip. But there are other ships.
They have cargo in them never intended to be carried only
from New York to New Jersey. There are engines in them
never meant merely to cross the river with. Size and tonnage
and fuel are there that ferryboats do not need. They are seagoing ships; they could do business in great waters. So one
feels about the great souls. So the disciples felt about Christ.
"Death," they said, "hath no . . . dominion over him."

When Christ died on Calvary it was to the disciples as
though the sun had set. He had been to them glorious, but
now the black night crept up around him; his light was
quenched and the sun went down in darkness. Yes, but seeing
the sunset is altogether a matter of our point of view, relative
to our position on this revolving planet. Nothing happens to
the sun; it still is there; it will rise again. So the disciples felt
about Christ. The great souls of the race have always brought,

in man's deepest hours, the strong assurance of death's limited domain. There must be in them something eternal.

I am not arguing for immortality this Easter morning. I am saying, rather, that we have many good arguments against it. How could it be otherwise in this mysterious universe? The very idea of life after death raises a thousand questions. But they are upon the surface of our minds; they are our artificial constructs; we devise them with our wits. When, however, the great hours come—when some dearly loved soul passes from the world seen into the world unseen, or when the spectacle of personality's cost and value, its promise and possibility unfolds before us, or when the great souls shining upon us, like the sun, set in the west—then there it is once more, that inextinguishable flame of hope, that voice that like a bell, beyond our power to stop, tolls in the heart of man: "This corruptible must put on incorruption, and this mortal must put on immortality."

From one more major source rises this deathless hope— not alone from the way we ourselves are constituted, nor from our love of other people, but from our personal fellowship with God. One almost hesitates thus to use the word God, meaning our Unseen Friend within, the Spiritual Presence there, for fear that someone here may feel himself shut out, not knowing what fellowship with God may mean. But if we think of God as the New Testament does, we all must know that inner companionship. "God is love," says John. He is not adequately pictured as a sovereign figure on a throne or in terms of cosmic creatorhood, omnipotent and omniscient. God is closer at hand than that. He is love, yes, and goodness, beauty, truth, so that wherever such spiritual experiences are, there God is, too, not far off but near, not outside us but within. That is where we really meet God—within ourselves. "Know ye not that ye are a temple of God, and that the Spirit of God dwelleth in you?"

In this deep sense no one, not even if he calls himself an

atheist, escapes the presence of God, for while our theories of life may be materialistic, our profoundest experiences are never materialistic—never! All our great hours—when beauty comes to us, or love, or goodness, or truth, or when duty calls and power within rises to meet it—are spiritual, through and through.

Say this to yourself this Easter: We are inhabitants now of a spiritual world invisible. We need not wait for death to introduce us to that experience. Now we dwell in a world of spirit, unseen and unseeable. No one ever saw an idea or an ideal, or a love or a truth. No one ever saw a thought or the mind that thought it. No one ever saw himself—not his real self; nor his friend—not his friend's spirit. The deepest forces in our lives are now invisible and spiritual. Across the centuries no experience has been more universal than the sense of Someone greater than ourselves dwelling with us, but no one ever saw that Divine Presence. See how true it is that our materialistic theories about life are on the surface of our minds, but our realistic experiences of life are spiritual, in a world within, unseen and unseeable. So, when the great hours come there it is again, that deathless hope of life beyond the grave. For what has death to do with this relationship between our souls and the world invisible? Why should death sever that tie, binding our spirits to our God? When Whittier sings,

> . . . warm, sweet, tender, even yet
> A present help is he,

he speaks of a vital companionship between man's soul and the Oversoul. When the Master says, "I am not alone, but I and the Father," he voices an experience profound and real. That essential experience of great religion is too universal to be denied, and when the great hours come there rises from it an affirmation that every one of us has felt the force of, however we may have tried to withstand it. "The souls of the righteous are in the hand of God."

The real difference, therefore, between us who sit here now is not that some of us thoroughly believe in life eternal and some of us thoroughly disbelieve it. In the depths of our souls every one of us believes it more or less, sometimes, at least once in a while, in the great hours. The difference between us lies rather in the fact that some of us are dealing with that immortal hope as though we tried to play with one finger, on a piano, the Easter hymn we just have sung—thinly, hesitantly, with no sweep and power—while others deal with it as an orchestra might play it—as Paul plays it in this triumphant chapter of I Corinthians—with confidence and certainty. Well, we seldom go wrong if we trust the deepest things in us, and nothing is deeper in us than this deathless hope that Easter celebrates. Out of the profoundest qualities that make us what we are, out of our love for the dearest, noblest persons we have known, out of our innermost companionship with the world Divine and invisible, this deathless hope arises. Our ways of picturing life after death cannot be adequate or true, but in its substance that hope is not mistaken. In the strength of it go out to face this world of war and turmoil! The Lord God Omnipotent reigneth still, and death shall be swallowed up in victory!